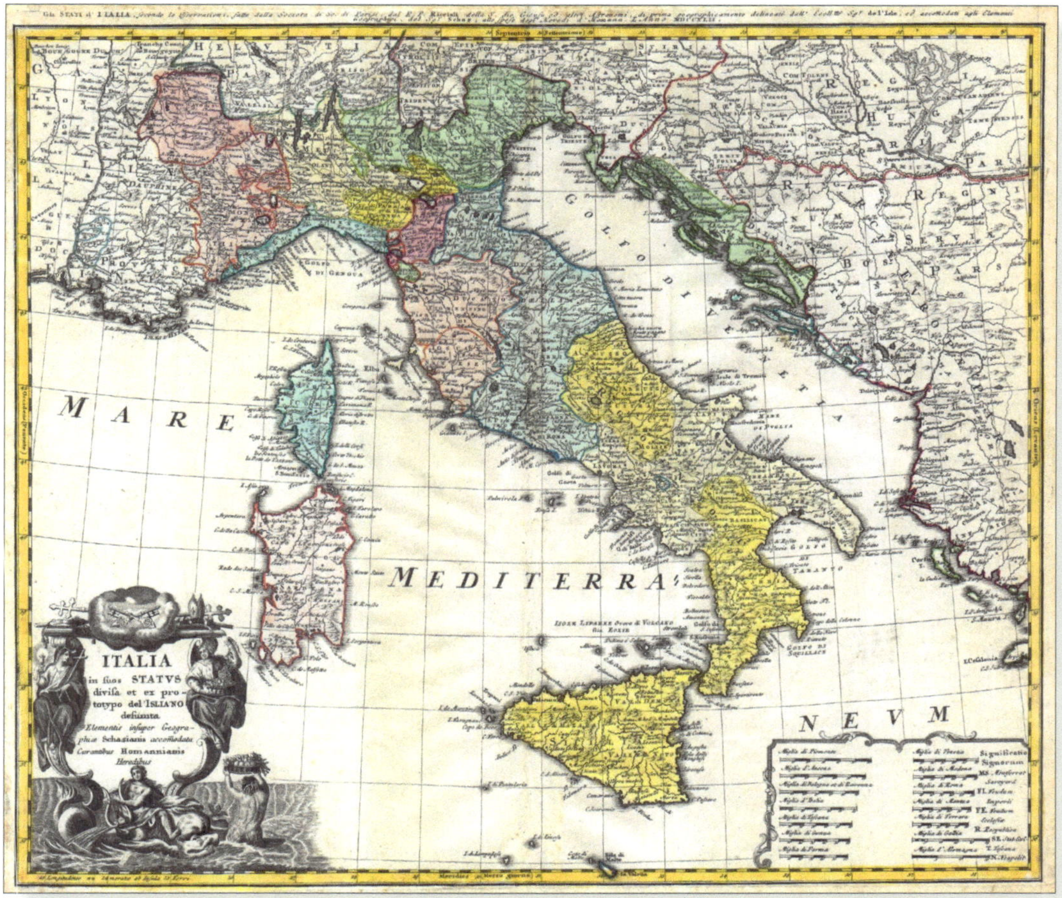
ITALIA
in suos STATVS
divisa et ex pro-
totypo del ISLIANO
definita.
MARE
MEDITERRA
NEVM

PUBLISHING'S NOTE
None of **unpublished** images or text of our book may be reproduced in any format without the expressed written permission of Soldiershop.com when not indicate as marked with license creative commons 3.0 or 4.0. The publisher remains to disposition of the possible having right for all the doubtful sources images or not identifies. Our trademark: Soldiershop Publishing ©, The names of our series: Soldiers&Weapons, Battlefield, War in colour, PaperSoldiers, Soldiershop e-book etc. are herein © by Soldiershop.com.

NOTE ABOUT BOOK PRINTING BEFORE 1929
This book may contain text or images coming from a reproduction of a book published before 1925 (over seventy years ago). No effort has been made to modernize or standardize the spelling used in the original text, so this book may have occasional imperfections such as missing or blurred pages, poor pictures, errant marks, etc. that were either part of the original artifact, or were introduced by the scanning process. We believe this work is culturally important, and despite the imperfections, have elected to bring it back into print (digital and/or paper) as part of our continuing commitment to the preservation of printed works worldwide. We appreciate your understanding of the imperfections in the preservation process, and hope you enjoy this valuable book. Now this book is purpose re-built and is proof-read and re-type set from the original to provide an outstanding experience of reflowing text, also for an ebook reader. However Soldiershop publishing added, enriched, revised and overhauled the text, images, etc. of the cover and the book. Therefore, the job is now to all intents and purposes a derivative work, and the added, new and original parts of the book are the copyright of Soldiershop. On this second unpublished part of the book none of images or text may be reproduced in any format without the expressed written permission of Soldiershop. Almost many of the images of our books and prints are taken from original first edition prints or books that are no longer in copyright and are therefore public domain. We have been a specialized bookstore for a long time so we (and several friends antiquarian booksellers) have readily available a lot of ancient, historical and illustrated books not in copyright. Each of our prints, art designs or illustrations is either our own creation, or a fully digitally restoration by our computer artists, or non copyrighted images. All of our prints are "tagged" with a registered digital copyright. Soldiershop remains to disposition of the possible having right for all the doubtful sources images or not identifies.

LICENSES COMMONS
This book may utilize material marked with license creative commons 3.0 or 4.0 (CC BY 4.0), (CC BY-ND 4.0), (CC BY-SA 4.0) or (CC0 1.0). We give appropriate attribution credit and indicate if change were made below in the acknowledgments field. All our Museum books utilize only fonts licensed under the SIL Open Font License or other free use license.

ACKNOWLEDGMENTS
A Special Thanks to Rijksmuseum of Amsterdam which provided most of the prints showed next. And at all the other institutions for their kindly permission to use some images of his archives, collections or books used in our book.

Title: **CIVITATES ORBIS TERRARUM** by Luca S. Cristini & Anna Cristini
First edition by Luca Cristini Editore June 2019
Cover & Art Design: Luca S. Cristini. ISBN code: 9788893274739
Published by Luca Cristini Editore, via Orio 35/4- 24050 Zanica (BG) ITALY. http://bookmuseum.it/
Code.: **MUSEUM-011**, Editorial series code: **H&T-002**
MUSEUM book is a trademark of Luca Cristini Editore

CIVITATES ORBIS TERRARUM

FROM THE RENAISSANCE PRINTS OF BRAUN AND HOGENBERG
DALLE STAMPE RINASCIMENTALI DI BRAUN E HOGENBERG

LUCA STEFANO CRISTINI & ANNA CRISTINI

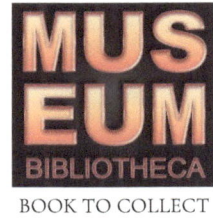

Cover of the first volume of *Civitates Orbis Terrarum* by Georg Braun, 1572
Copertina del primo volume del Civitates Orbis Terrarum *di Georg Braun, 1572*

THE RISE OF MODERN CARTOGRAPHY

Long before we could remotely assume the existence of satellites capable of providing detailed images of the entire planet, at any time and in any place, there were cartographers who responded to humans' natural need to discover the world around them. The 16th century was the height of "travel literature", an extremely attractive genre for a public that, bewitched by new geographical discoveries and explorations, wished to travel without having to leave its home and thus avoid facing the dangers that usually conditioned travels at the time.

Modern cartography, as we understand it today, was born a little earlier in reality, in the prolific second half of the 15th century, as a consequence mainly of three factors: the recovery of Ptolemy's work, the invention of printing and the above mentioned discoveries overseas. Claudius Ptolemy (2nd century AD) was without a doubt one of the most influential geographers of antiquity; not only that, his discoveries in astronomy and astrology led him to hold an important position in the Prefecture of Egypt of the Roman Empire. His most famous work, the *Almagest*, survived several centuries until the Arabs finally introduced it to Europe. In the paper was collected almost all the astronomical knowledge of the period and at the same time the author introduced his vision of the solar model, which was called the Ptolemaic system, which became a reference point for navigators of the Western world and beyond, until it was replaced by the heliocentric system of Niccolò Copernico. The *Almagest* was then translated into Latin, correcting also some topographical errors, including the greatness of the Mediterranean Sea, giving rise to the *"Tabulae Modernae"*, the first printed maps, between 1420 and 1465. This was possible thanks to the invention of the movable typeface printing of 1454, by Johannes Gutenberg. Before him, in fact, the high cost of manuscripts restricted access to geographical culture to noble kings and shipping companies.

The first navigators left Portugal to discover the African coasts, till crossing the Cape of Good Hope and entering the Pacific. At the same time, in Sagres, the city considered "o fin do mundo" before then, the school of cartography was born together with Martin Behaim, German merchant, astronomer and geographer who, in 1492 and thanks to the discovery of America, created the first preserved globe, the so-called Erdapfel (in German, "apple of the earth").

With Christopher Columbus and the expedition of Magellan (1519-1520) who first circumnavigated the world, the cartographers of the 16th century began to reveal more complete and complex maps; from that moment on, the scientific accuracy and the exactness of the places and borders represented assumed vital importance, and the master cartographers were no longer the navigators themselves, but the mathematicians and astronomers who travelled with them, mostly Germans and Flemish. Instruments that had been useful for calculating latitude up to that point, such as the astrolabe or the quadrant, were simplified with the nautical astrolabe and Jacob's stick. In 1571 the English mathematician Leonard Digges presented the planchette, an instrument that allowed the creation of the map simultaneously with the tracking of navigation angles. The calculation of longitude was more complicated at the time. The method of lunar distances and the chronometer were useless without knowing, for example, the different positions of the moon in relation to the stars in the different meridians, but for that we will have to wait about two centuries.

At the same time as the discovery of new boundaries, the relative maps were being created, in many cases revisitations of works by the aforementioned Ptolemy. At the turn of the 16th and 17th centuries, around fifty editions of the *Geographia* were produced, which differed slightly depending on the cartographer in charge and the place of origin of the author. But the Ptolemaic re-editions were soon accompanied by unedited works such as the famous *Theatrum Orbis Terrarum* (1570) by Abraham Ortelius, which became the reference text in terms of maps and panoramic views of the various cities around the world known until now. The author had collected in one work the best available maps made by the best cartographers around and the success was such that it was quickly translated and distributed in several languages. A few years later, a canon from Cologne Cathedral would have laid the foundations for an editorial plan that lasted a total of forty years and that represented the first urban atlas in history.

Georg Braun was born in Cologne in 1541 from the glassmaker Tilmann Bruin and began his theological studies until he became canon and rector of the church of Santa Maria Gradus, in his hometown. From 1572, however, he decided to dedicate himself to a job to which he would devote half of his life: the *Civitates Orbis Terrarum* (translated into English as "the cities of the world") initially conceived as a complementary project to the cited *Theatrum* and inspired by the *Cosmographia* of Sebastian Münster.

Portrait of Abraham Ortelius by Rubens, Plantin-Moretusmuseum of Antwerp
Abraham Ortelius, ritratto da Rubens, Complesso museale di Plantin-Moretus di Anversa

Completed in 1617 with the publication of the sixth and last volume, the work contains 546 perspectives, bird's eye views and maps of the cities of (almost) the whole world. At first only European cities were considered, but with the different editions over time we see how exotic places from overseas, such as the mystical city of Cuzco or Mexico City, begin to make their way through Mumbai and Goa; city views are generally reported in double pages inside, while the respective historical and topographical descriptions are printed on the outside.

Hyerosolyma, the city of Jerusalem appears in the second volume of *Civitates Orbis Terrarum*
Hyerosolyma, la città di Gerusalemme appare nel secondo volume del *Civitates Orbis Terrarum*

Braun used a large team of collaborators to make his work, but he was the only one still alive to see the publication of the last volume. As an author, in fact, he undertook only a few trips out of his Germany, taking on the task of maintaining extensive contacts with people more akin to long expeditions, and taking care entirely of the part relating to the texts. Frans Hogenberg made most of the printing plates, along with his son Abraham and Simon Van den Neuwel, while Georg Hoefnagel was the Dutch painter in charge of composing the live panoramic views of the cities; it was he who made most of the journeys necessary for the creation of this vast atlas.

As for the textual part edited by Braun -written almost entirely in Latin- he focused on the history of the city and its socio-economic position. The social slant adopted by the author is interesting: the intrinsic intention was to represent the civilized world thanks to and through the city, now understood as a system. An authentic historical taxonomy of medieval and Renaissance urbanism, probably a legacy of the ecclesiastical formation of Georg Braun; he died in Cologne in 1622 at the age of eighty, being the only original participant in the project still alive to see the publication of the sixth volume five years earlier.

Undoubtedly the *Civitates Orbis Terrarum*, together with the *Theatrum Orbis Terrarum*, responded to a growing interest from Europeans in the knowledge of the time, and they did so following a rigor and a geographical and artistic accuracy never seen before. This interest also arose at a time when the purchasing power was definitely increasing in certain social classes and, as already mentioned a few lines above, the price of printed books was much more affordable than previous books produced by the scribes. The success of these first two atlases was such that no one would consider other works of this kind throughout the next century, not bad as the first ancestral prototype of Google Earth.

In this first volume dedicated to *Civitates Orbis Terrarum* are reported the 80 plates describing Italy, from north to south, and following the navigation through the Mediterranean Sea's costs. Flipping through the pages that follow, it is possible to recognize familiar cities and towns, but are you ready to discover their appearance five centuries ago?

All we can do is wishing you a pleasant journey.

The world seen by Claudius Ptolemy in 150 AD
Il mondo visto da Claudio Tolomeo nel 150 d.C.

NASCITA DELLA CARTOGRAFIA MODERNA

Molto prima che si potesse remotamente ipotizzare l'esistenza di satelliti in grado di fornire immagini dettagliate dell'intero pianeta, in ogni istante e in ogni luogo, erano i cartografi che rispondevano alla naturale esigenza dell'uomo di conoscere il mondo circondante. Il XVI secolo rappresentò l'apice della "letteratura da viaggio", un genere estremamente attraente per un pubblico che, ammaliato dalle nuove scoperte geografiche ed esplorazioni, desiderava viaggiare senza dover abbandonare la propria casa e dunque evitare di affrontare i pericoli che di solito condivano i viaggi all'epoca.

La cartografia moderna come la intendiamo al giorno d'oggi nasce un po' prima in realtà, nella prolifica seconda metà del 1400, come conseguenza principalmente di tre fattori: il recupero dell'opera di Tolomeo, l'invenzione della stampa e le sopraccitate scoperte oltreoceano. Claudio Tolomeo (II secolo d.C.) è stato senza ombra di dubbio uno dei geografi più influenti dell'antichità; non solo, le sue scoperte in ambito astronomico e astrologico lo portarono a ricoprire una posizione importante nella Prefettura d'Egitto dell'Impero Romano. La sua opera più famosa, l'*Almagesto*, sopravvisse vari secoli fino a che gli arabi la introdussero finalmente in Europa. Nello scritto veniva raccolta quasi tutta la conoscenza astronomica dell'epoca e al tempo stesso l'autore introduceva la propria visione del modello solare, che prese il nome di sistema tolemaico, divenuto punto di riferimento per navigatori del mondo occidentale e non, fino a che venne sostituito con il sistema eliocentrico di Niccolò Copernico. L'*Almagesto* venne dunque tradotto al latino correggendo anche alcuni errori topografici, tra cui la grandezza del Mar Mediterraneo, dando vita alle "*Tabulae Modernae*", le prime mappe stampate, a cavallo tra il 1420 e il 1465. Ciò fu possibile grazie all'invenzione della stampa a caratteri mobili del 1454, per mano di Johannes Gutenberg. Prima di lui, infatti, gli elevati costi dei manoscritti circoscrivevano di fatto l'accesso alla cultura geografica ai nobili re e alle compagnie di navigazione.

Cristopher Columbus portrayed by Sebastiano di Piombo in 1519
Cristoforo Colombo ritratto da Sebastiano di Piombo nel 1519

I primi navigatori partirono dal Portogallo alla scoperta delle coste africane, fino ad attraversare il Capo di Buona Speranza ed addentrandosi nel Pacifico. Contemporaneamente, a Sagres, la città considerata "o fin do mundo" prima di allora, nasce la scuola di cartografia insieme a Martin Behaim, commerciante, astronomo e geografo tedesco che nel 1492 e grazie alla scoperta dell'America, realizzò il primo mappamondo che si conserva, il cosiddetto *Erdapfel* (in tedesco, "mela della terra"). Con Cristoforo Colombo e la spedizione di Magellano (1519-1520) che per primo circumnavigò il mondo, i cartografi del secolo XVI cominciarono a produrre mappe più complete e complesse; da quel momento il rigore scientifico e l'esattezza dei luoghi e confini rappresentati assunsero una vitale importanza, e i maestri cartografi non erano più i navigatori stessi, bensì i matematici e gli astronomi che con loro viaggiavano, perlopiù tedeschi e fiamminghi. Gli strumenti sino a quel momento utili per il calcolo della latitudine, come l'astrolabio o il quadrante, si semplificano con l'astrolabio nautico e il bastone di Giacobbe. Nel 1571 il matematico inglese Leonard Digges presentò la planchette, uno strumento che permetteva la creazione della mappa simultanea al tracciamento degli angoli di navigazione. Il calcolo della longitudine presentava all'epoca maggiori complicazioni. Il metodo delle distanze lunari ed il cronometro risultavano inutili senza conoscere, per esempio, le diverse posizioni della luna in rapporto alle stelle nei diversi meridiani, ma per quello bisognerà attendere ancora circa due secoli.

Contemporaneamente alla scoperta di nuovi confini sorgevano quindi le relative mappe, in molti casi rivisitazioni di opere del già citato Tolomeo. A cavallo del XVI e XVII secolo vennero prodotte all'incirca cinquanta edizioni della *Geographia*, le quali differivano leggermente a seconda del cartografo responsabile e del luogo di provenienza dell'autore. Ma le riedizioni tolemaiche vennero presto accompagnate de opere inedite come il famoso *Theatrum Orbis Terrarum* (1570) di Abraham Ortelius, divenuto il testo di riferimento in quanto a mappe e viste panoramiche delle diverse città di tutto il mondo conosciuto sino ad ora. L'autore aveva raccolto in un'opera le migliori mappe disponibili realizzate dai migliori artisti cartografi in circolazione e il successo fu tale che fu rapidamente tradotto e distribuito in diverse lingue. Pochi anni dopo, un canonico della cattedrale di Colonia, avrebbe messo le basi per un piano editoriale durato complessivamente quarant'anni e che rappresentò il primo atlante urbano della storia.

Astrolabe and quadrant were the main tool for spatial mapping
L'astrolabio e il quadrante, strumenti indispensabili per le rilevazioni territoriali

Georg Braun nasce a Colonia nel 1541 dal vetraio Tilmann Bruin e inizia i suoi studi di teologia fino ad arrivare a ricoprire il ruolo di canonico e rettore della chiesa di Santa Maria Gradus, nella sua città natale. Dal 1572 tuttavia decide di dedicarsi a un lavoro cui avrebbe dedicato metà della sua vita: il *Civitates Orbis Terrarum* (traducibile in italiano come "le città del mondo) inizialmente concepito come progetto complementare al sopraccitato *Theatrum* ed ispirato alla *Cosmographia* di Sebastian Münster. Completata nel 1617 con la pubblicazione del sesto ed ultimo volume, l'opera contiene 546 prospettive, viste a volo d'uccello e mappe delle città di (quasi) tutto il mondo. Dapprima furono prese in considerazione solo città europee, ma con le diverse edizioni nel tempo vediamo come iniziano a farsi strada luoghi esotici da oltre oceano, come la mistica città di Cuzco o Città del Messico, passando per Mumbai e Goa; le vedute delle città sono generalmente riportate in doppie pagine all'interno, mentre le rispettive descrizioni storiche e topografiche sono stampate all'esterno. Braun si servì di una vasta squadra di collaboratori per realizzare la sua opera, ma fu l'unico ancora in vita a vedere la pubblicazione dell'ultimo volume. Come autore, infatti, intraprese solo pochi viaggi fuori dalla sua Germania incaricandosi piuttosto di mantenere contatti di vasta portata con gente più affine alle lunghe spedizioni, e curando interamente la parte relativa ai testi. Frans Hogenberg realizzò la maggior parte delle piastre per la stampa, insieme al figlio Abraham e a Simon Van den Neuwel, mentre Georg Hoefnagel fu il pittore olandese incaricato di comporre le viste panoramiche delle città, dal vivo; fu proprio lui a realizzare la maggior parte dei viaggi necessari alla creazione di questo vasto atlante. Per quanto riguarda la parte testuale curata da Braun –scritta quasi interamente in latino- questi si concentrò sulla storia della città e la relativa posizione socio-economico. Interessante è il taglio sociale adottato dall'autore: l'intenzione intrinseca era quella di rappresentare il mondo civilizzato grazie ed attraverso la città, intesa ormai come sistema. Un'autentica tassonomia storica dell'urbanismo medievale e rinascimentista, retaggio probabilmente della formazione ecclesiastica di Georg Braun; muore a Colonia nel 1622 all'età di ottant'anni, essendo l'unico dei partecipanti originali al progetto ancora in vita per vedere la pubblicazione del sesto volume cinque anni prima.

Indubbiamente il *Civitates Orbis Terrarum*, insieme al *Theatrum Orbis Terrarum*, rispondevano ad un crescente interesse da parte degli europei per la conoscenza del tempo, e lo facevano seguendo un rigore ed un'esattezza geografica e artistica mai visti prima. Quest'interesse nasce peraltro in un momento in cui il potere acquisitivo stava decisamente aumentando in determinate classi sociali e, come già accennato qualche riga più in su, il prezzo dei libri stampati era molto più accessibile dei precedenti libri prodotti dagli scrivani. Il successo di questi due primi atlanti fu tale che nessuno avrebbe preso in considerazione altre opere di questo genere per tutto il secolo successivo, non male come primo ancestrale prototipo di Google Earth.

In questo primo volume dedicato al *Civitates Orbis Terrarum* vengono riportate le 80 tavole che descrivono l'Italia, da nord a sud, e continuando con la navigazione fino alle coste del Mar Mediterraneo. Sfogliando le pagine che seguono è possibile riconoscere città e paesi familiari, ma siete pronti a scoprire il loro aspetto cinque secoli fa?

Non ci resta che augurarvi buon viaggio.

ITALY - ITALIA

ROMA

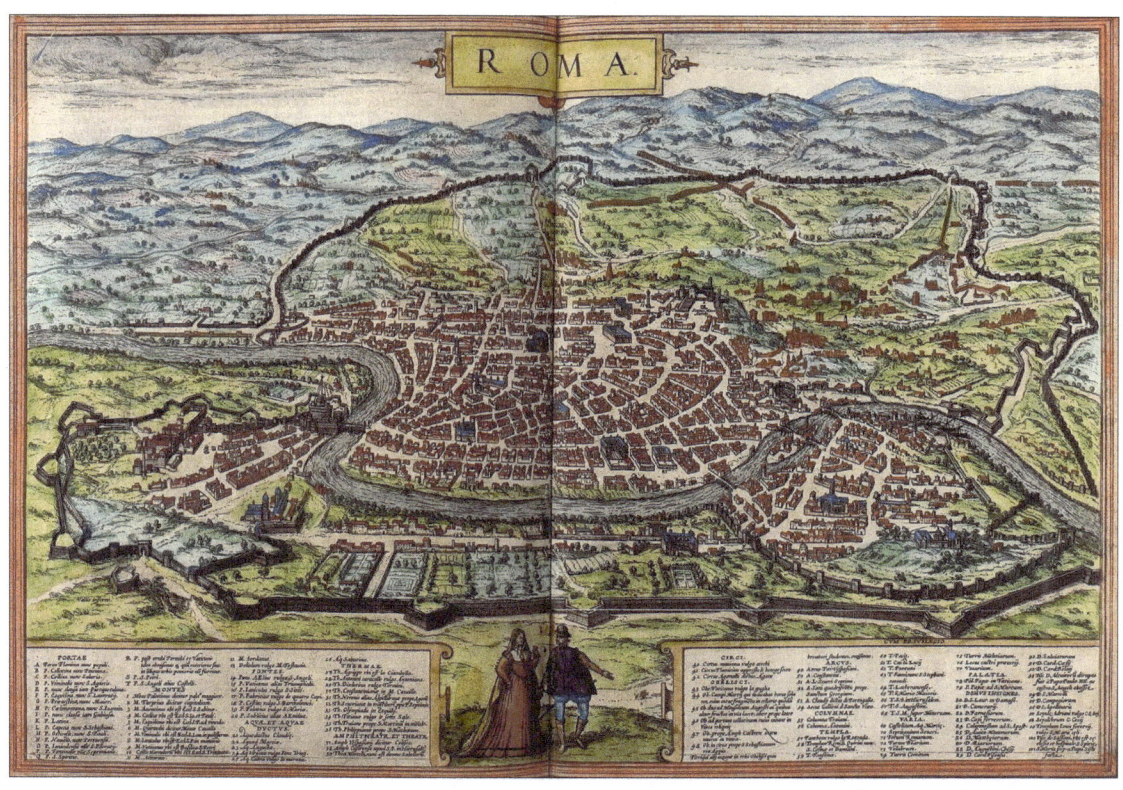
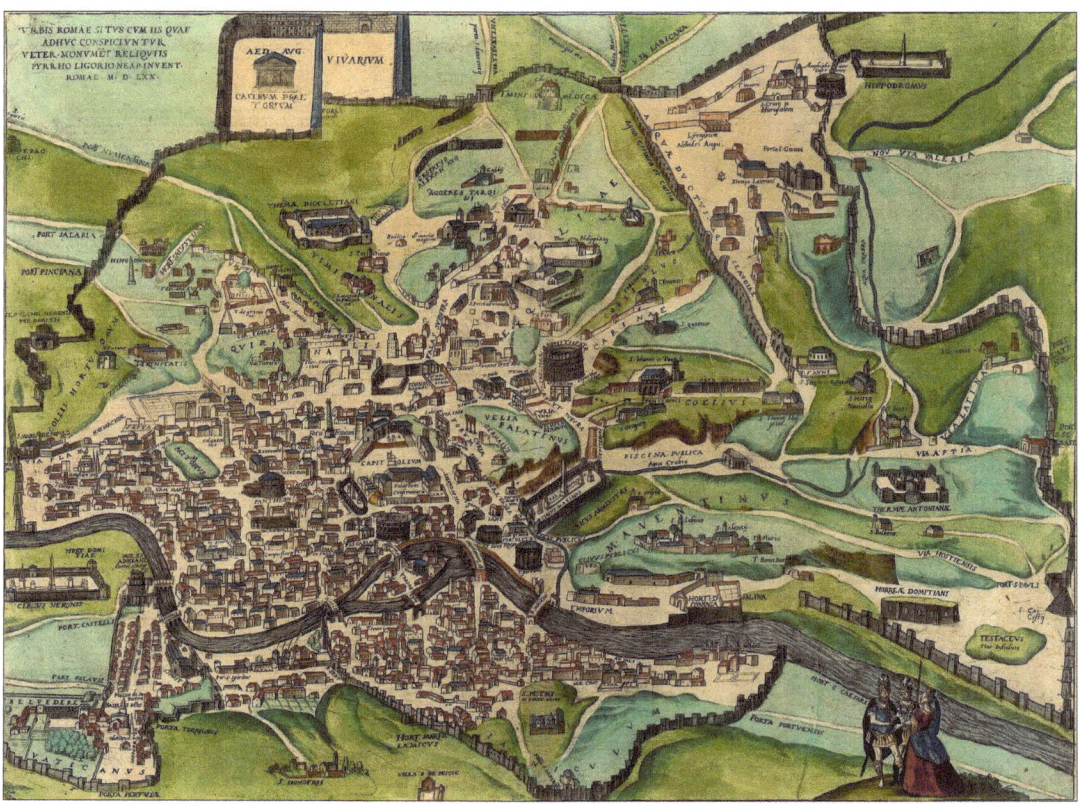

GENOVA - *Genua*

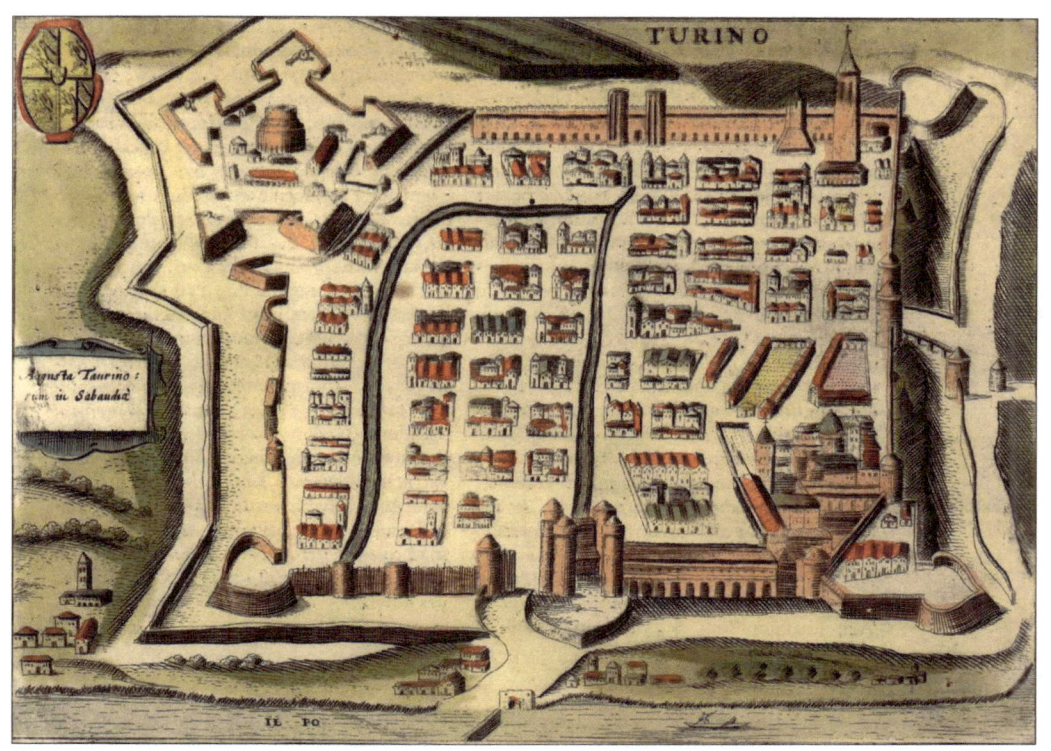
TORINO - *Turino*

TORTONA

CASALE MONFERRATO - *Cazal*

COMO - *Comum Duorum*

COIRA - *Chur*

TARVISIO - *Travisi*

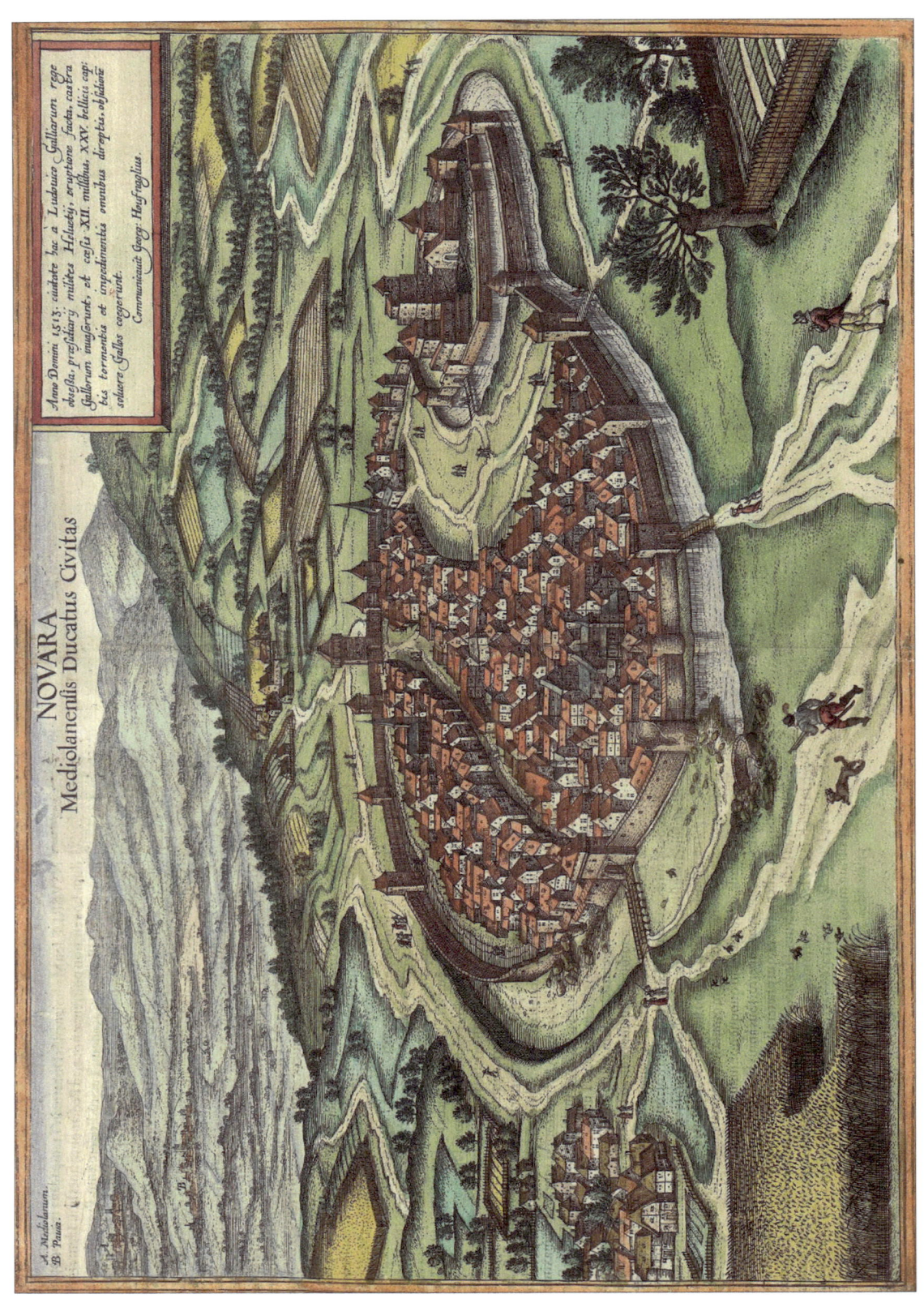

MILANO - *Mediolanum*

BERGAMO - *Bergomum*

BRESCIA - *Brixia*

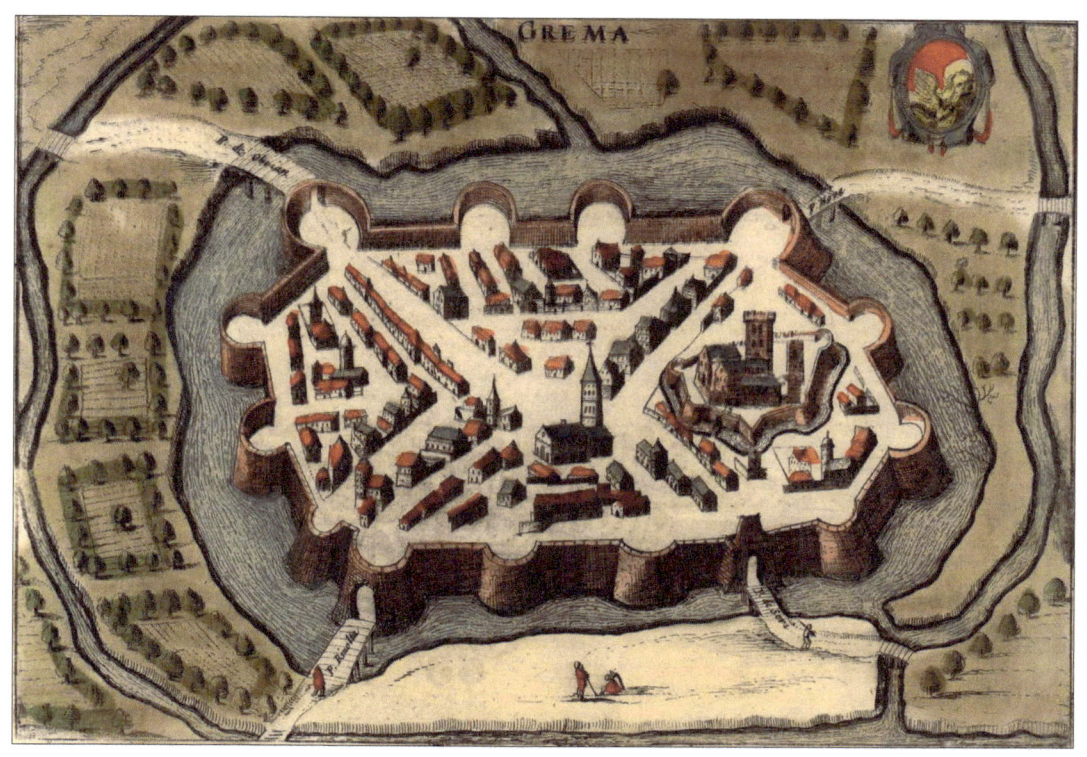

CREMA

CREMONA

PAVIA - *Ticinum*

MANTOVA - *Mantua*

VITTORIO VENETO - *Serravallum*

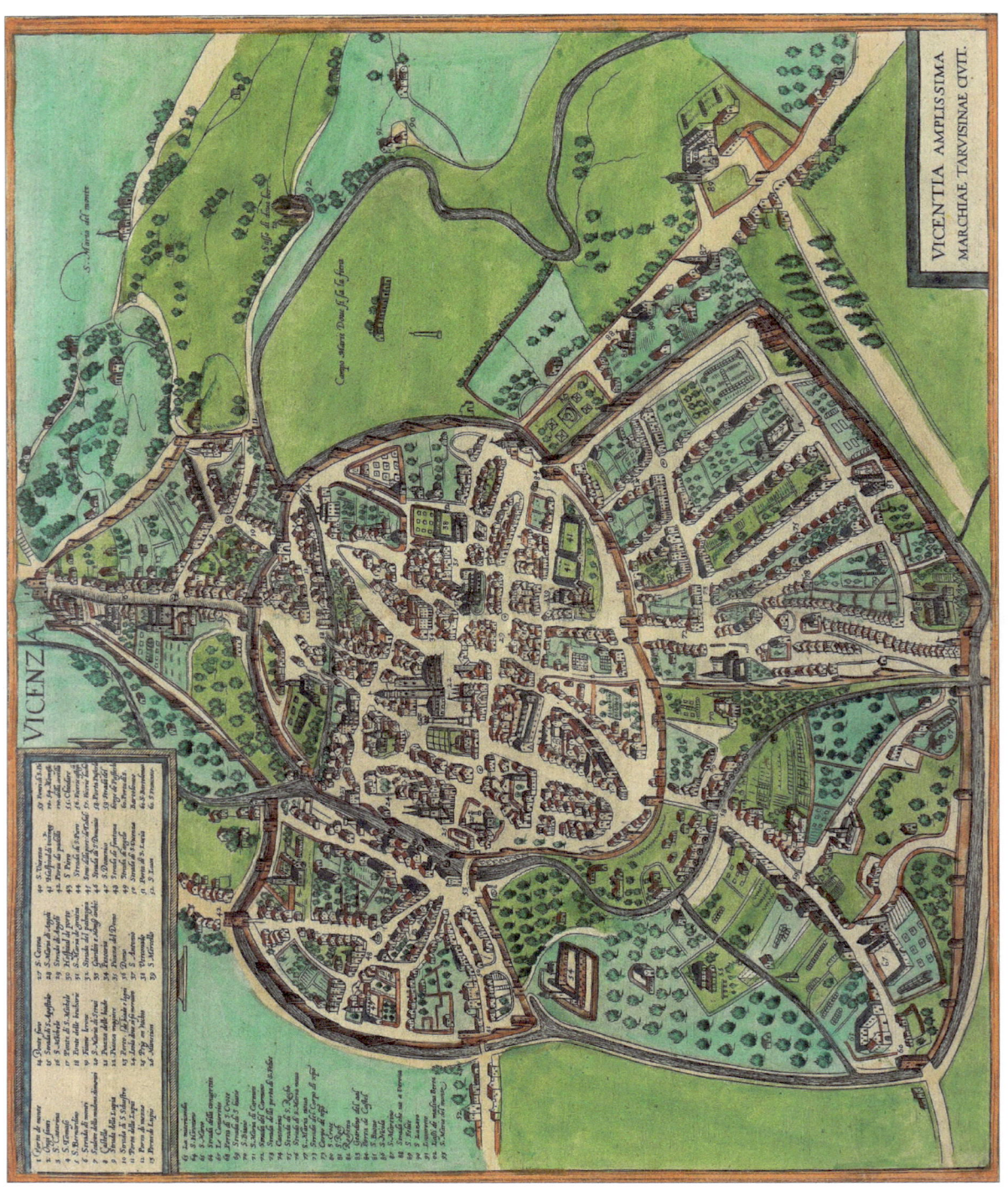

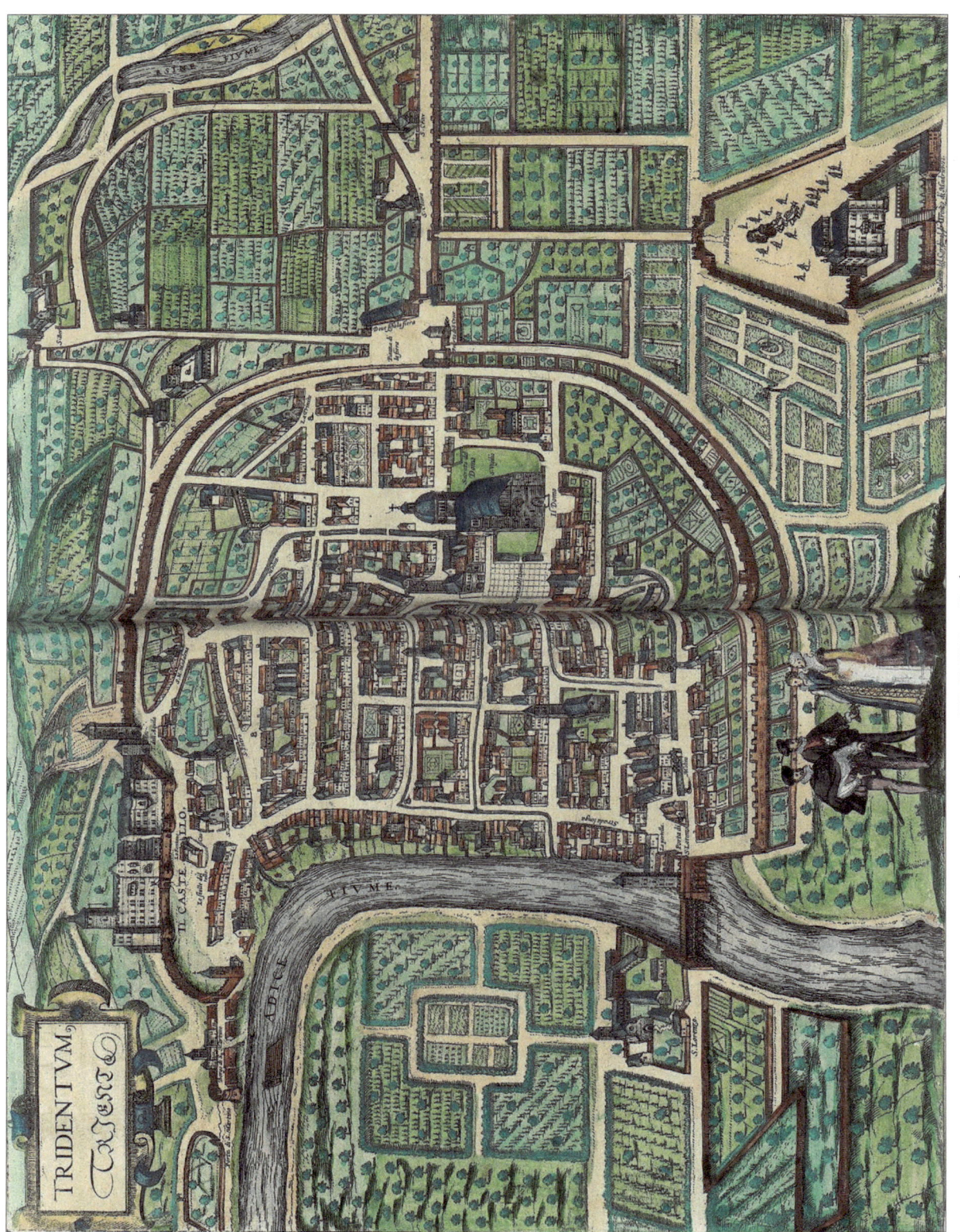

TRENTO - *Tridentum*

FORTE DI FUENTES - *Forte de Fontes*

UDINE - *Utinum*

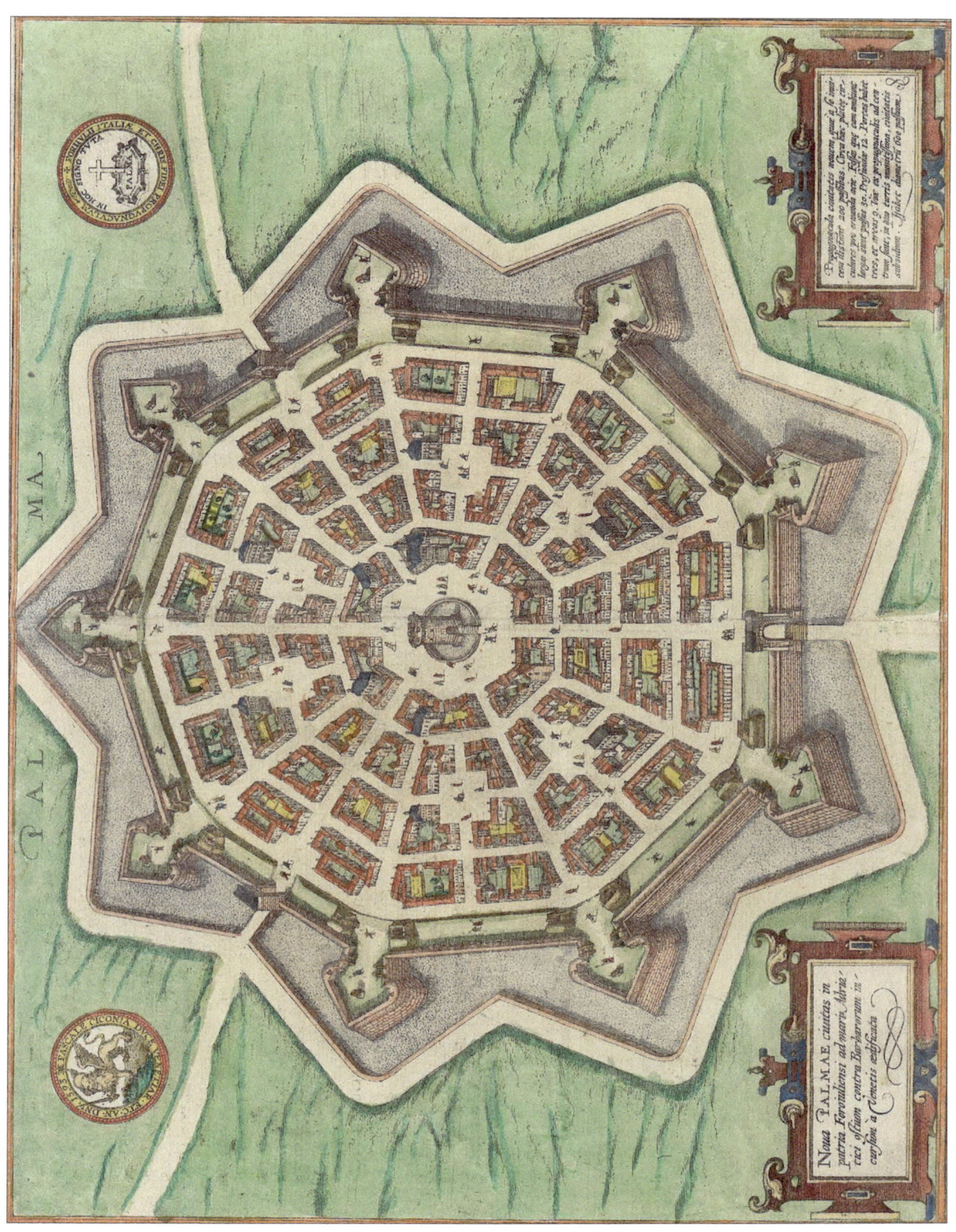

PALMANOVA - *Palma*

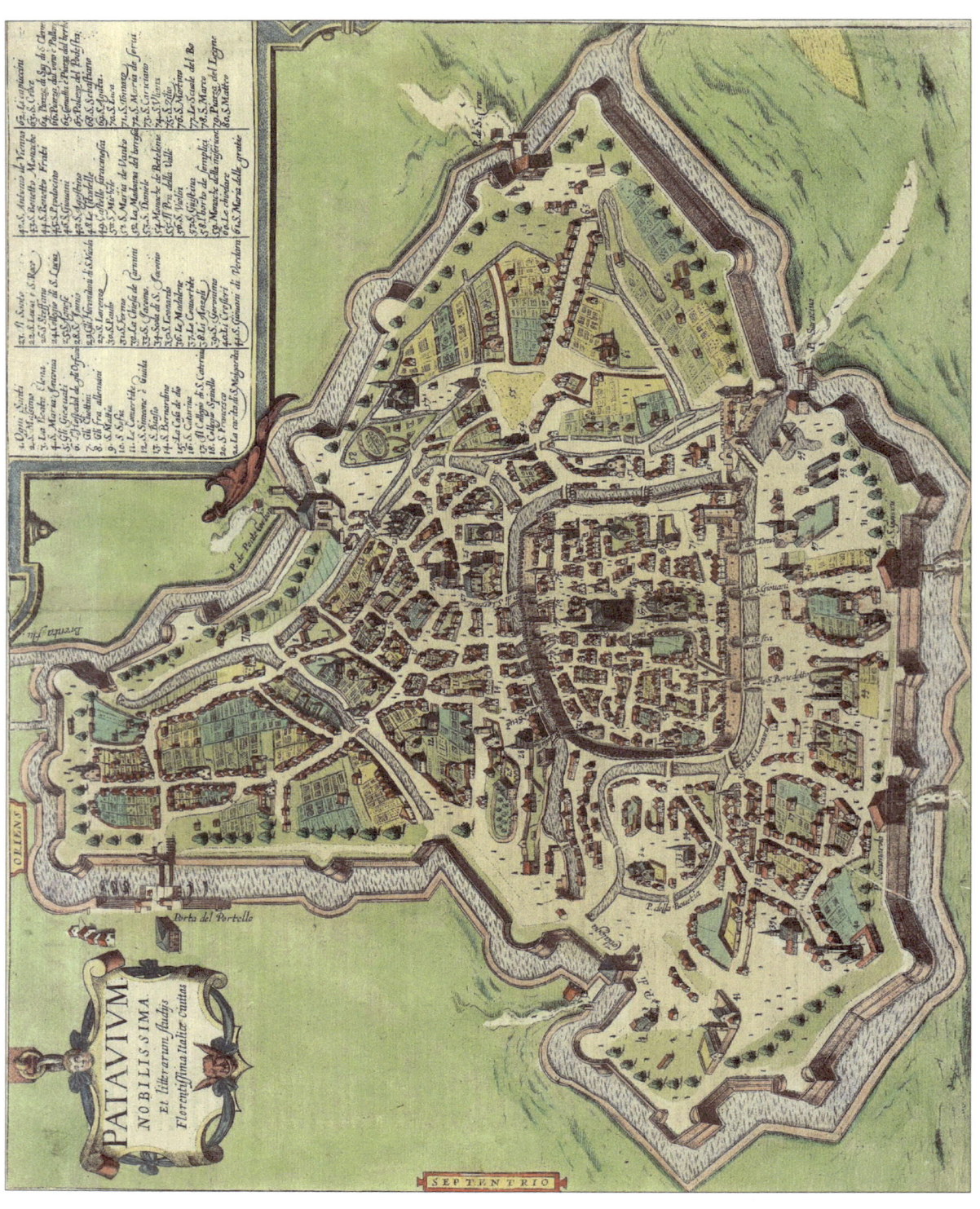

PADOVA - *Patavium*

MIRANDOLA

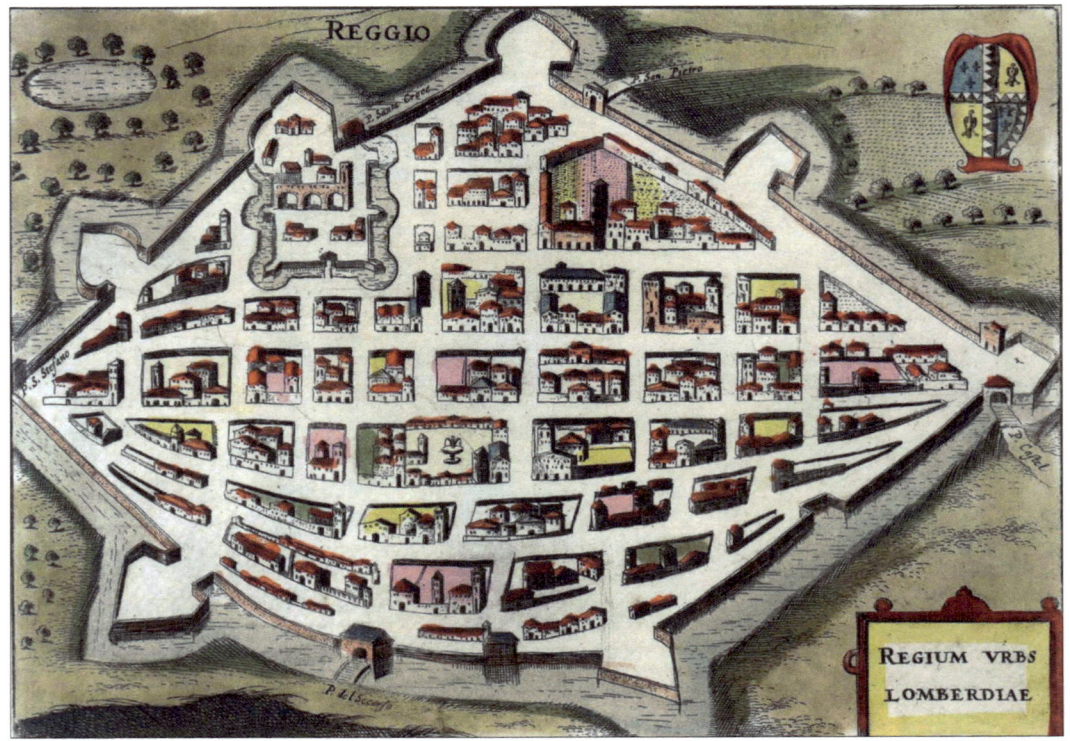

REGGIO EMILIA - *Regium*

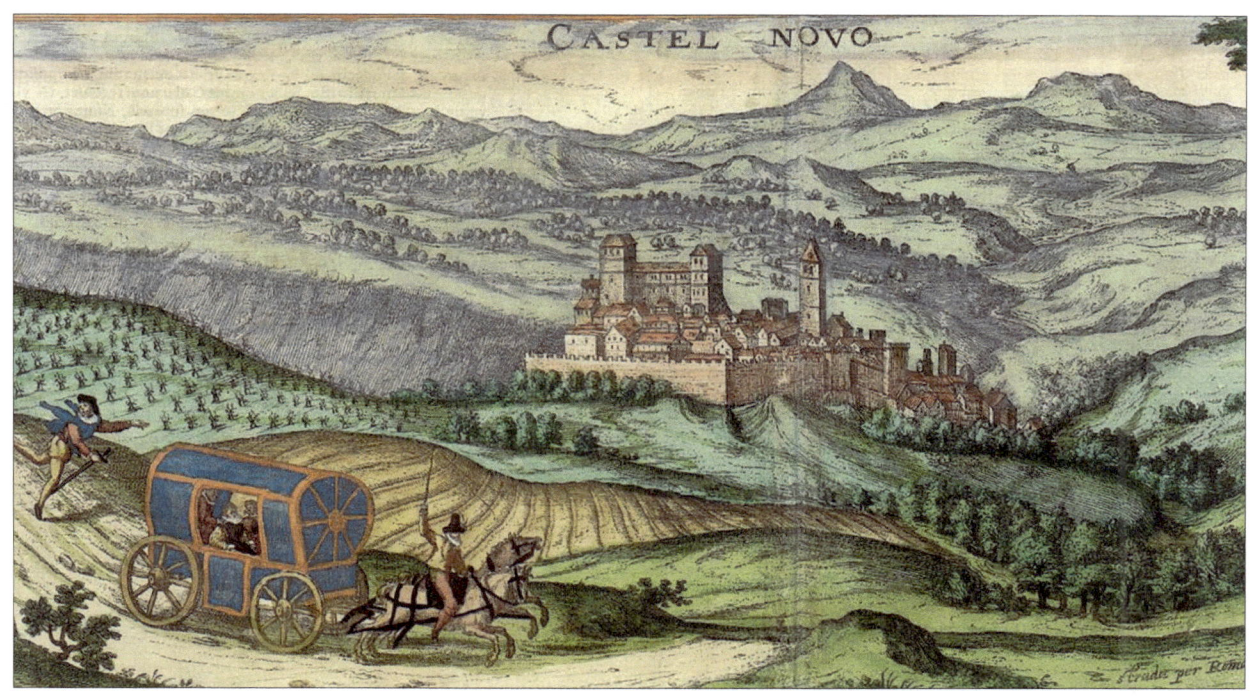

CASTELNOVO

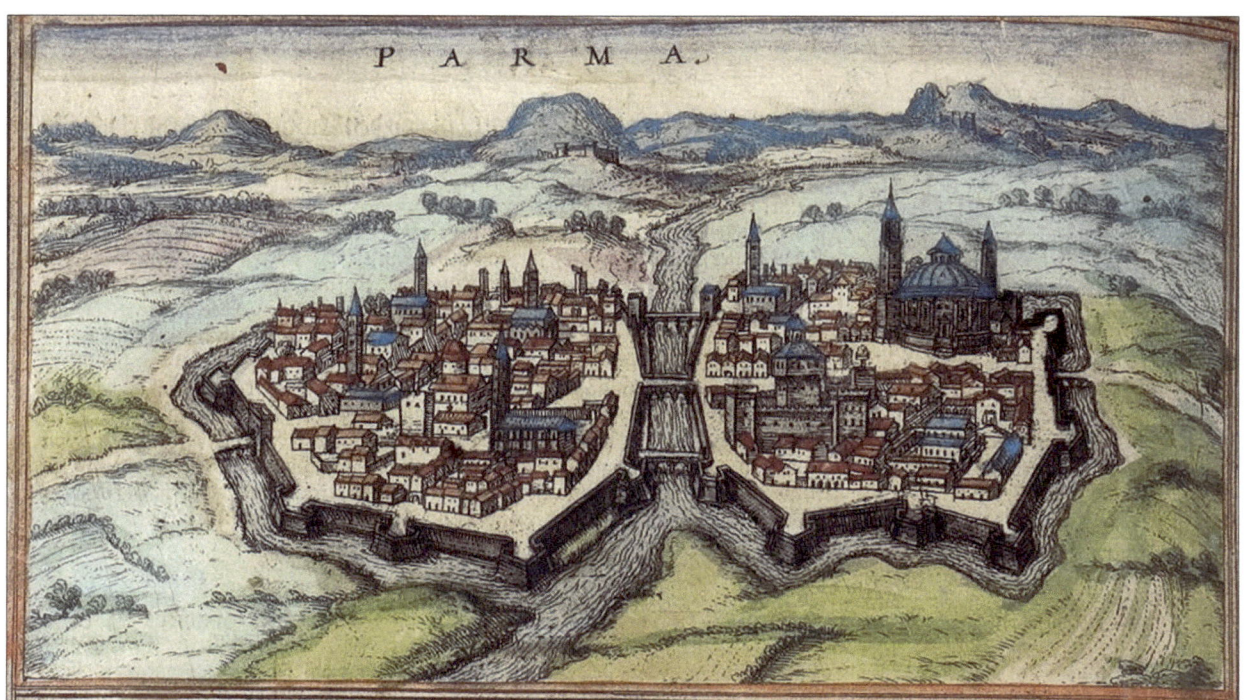

PARMA

PIACENZA - *Placentia*

BOLOGNA - *Bononia*

MASSA-CARRARA - *Montagna di Carara*

LUCCA - *Luca*

PISA

FIRENZE - *Florentia*

FLORENTIA urbs est insignis Hetruriæ, olim Fluentia dicta, quod
sita sit ad fluentum Arni fluminis. Et populi ipsi Fluentini, quorum memi:
nit Cato in originib: ut refert Angelus Politianus in quadam Epistola
ad Bartholomæum Scalam. Pulcherrimis tam publicis, quam priuatis orna:
ta ædificijs, et montibus undiq; septa, ex quibus, dictu mirum, quanta oblec
tatione visus in hanc urbem pandatur. Nobilium hominium sedes est, &
præstantissimorum ingenior. feracissimus ager

FLORENTIA

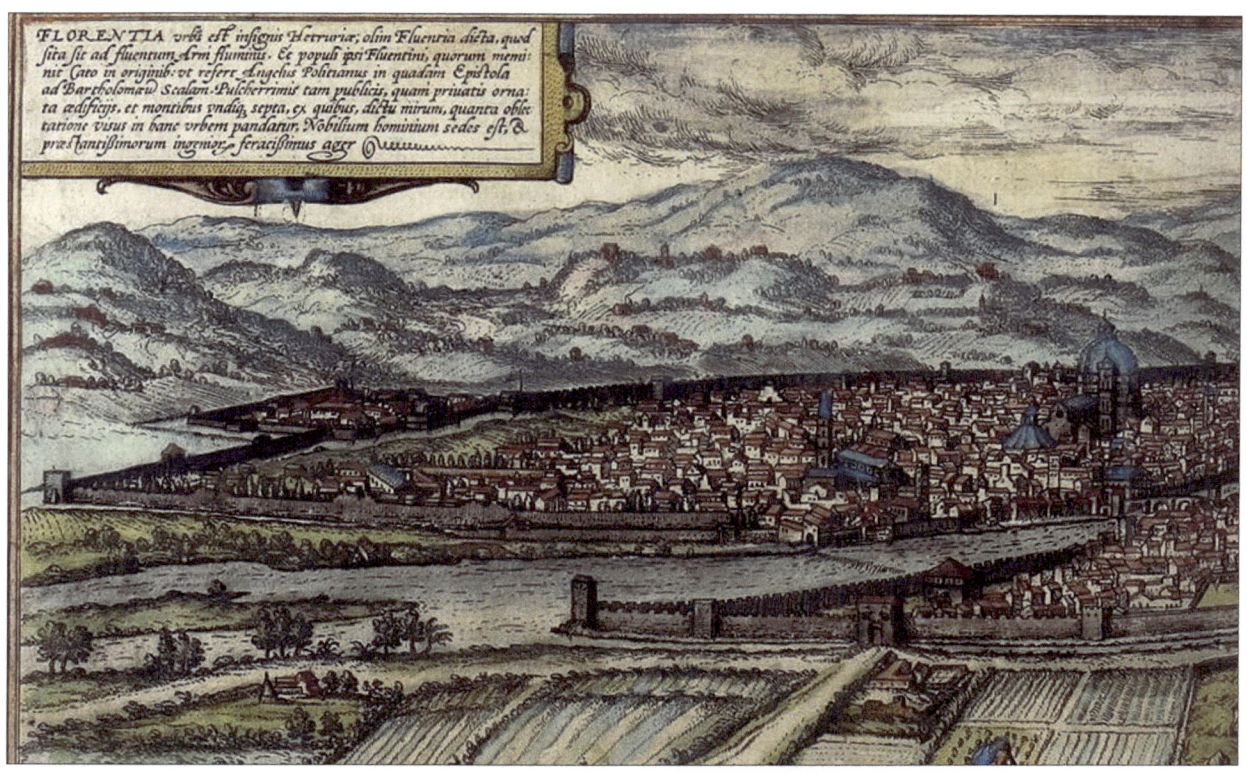

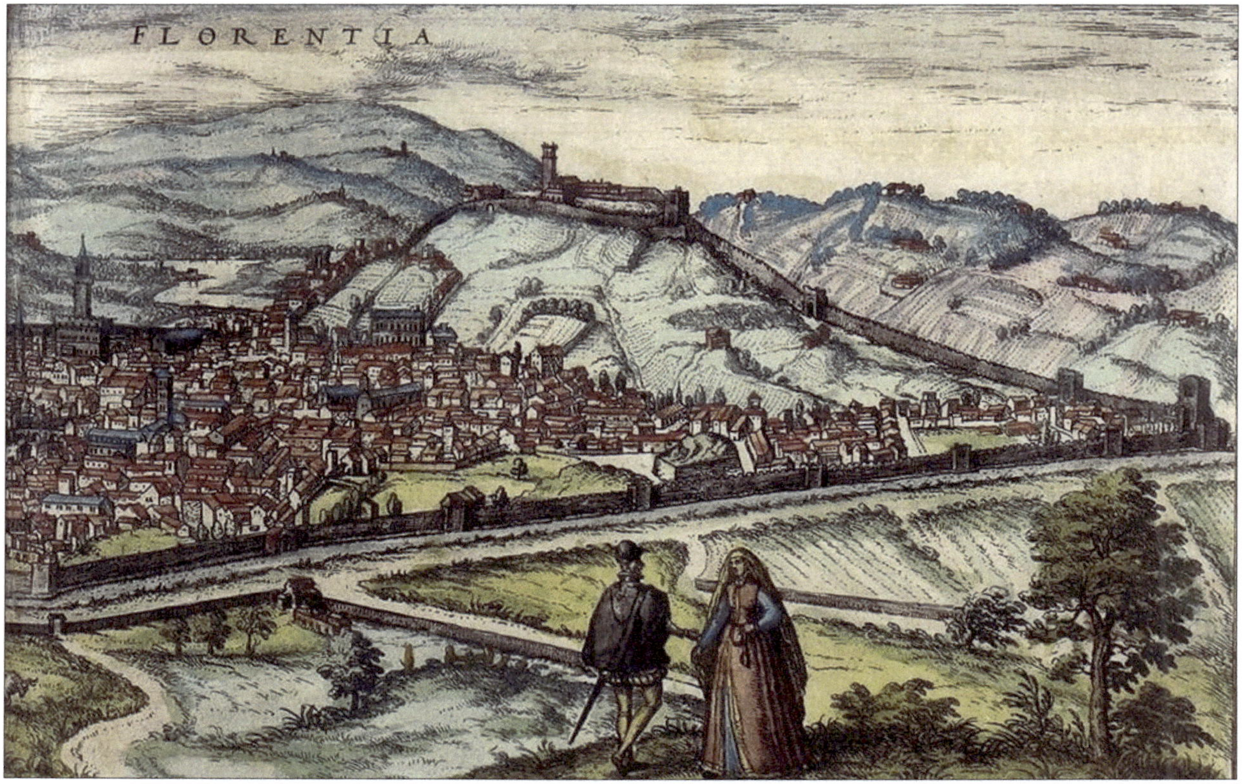

SIENA - *Sena*

SIENA

RADIOCOFANI - ASSISI

PESARO - *Pezaro*

URBINO

CAMERINO

ARCEVIA

ANCONA

LORETO - *Lauretum*

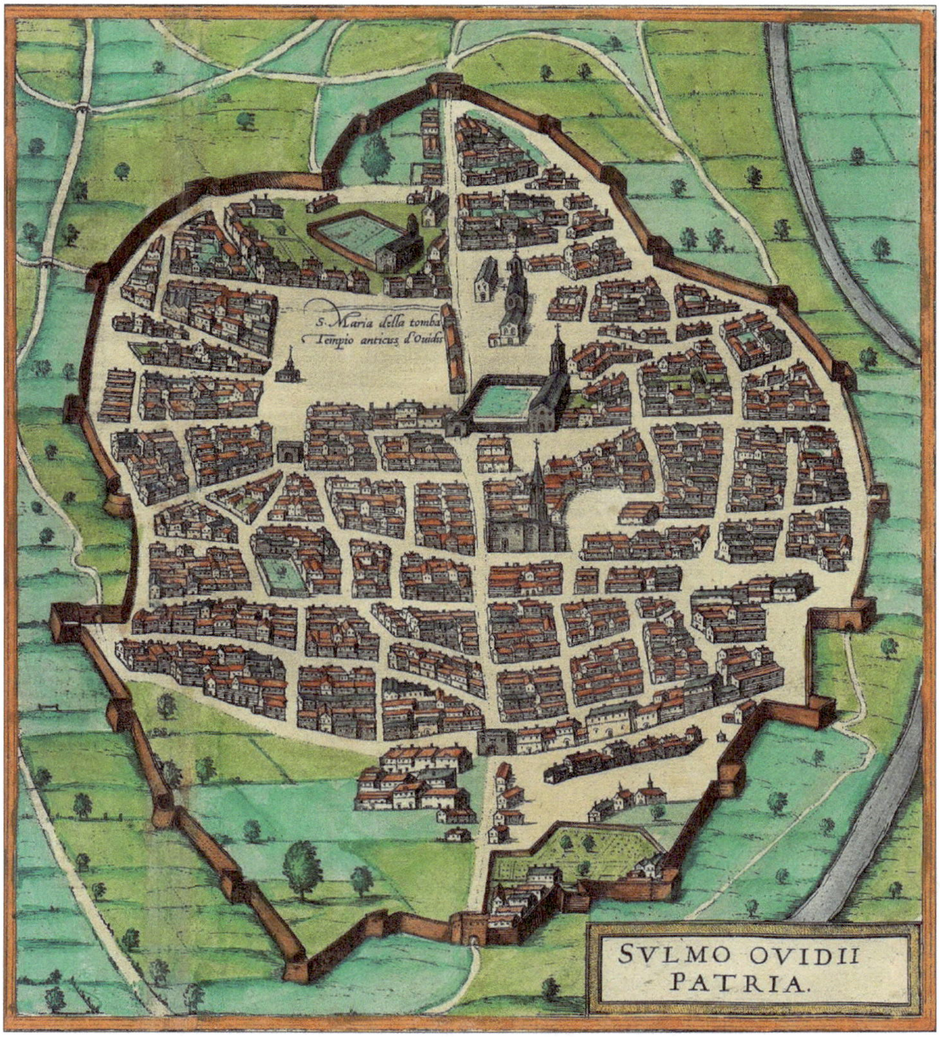

SULMONA - *Sulmo*

NOCERA UMBRA - *Nocerra*

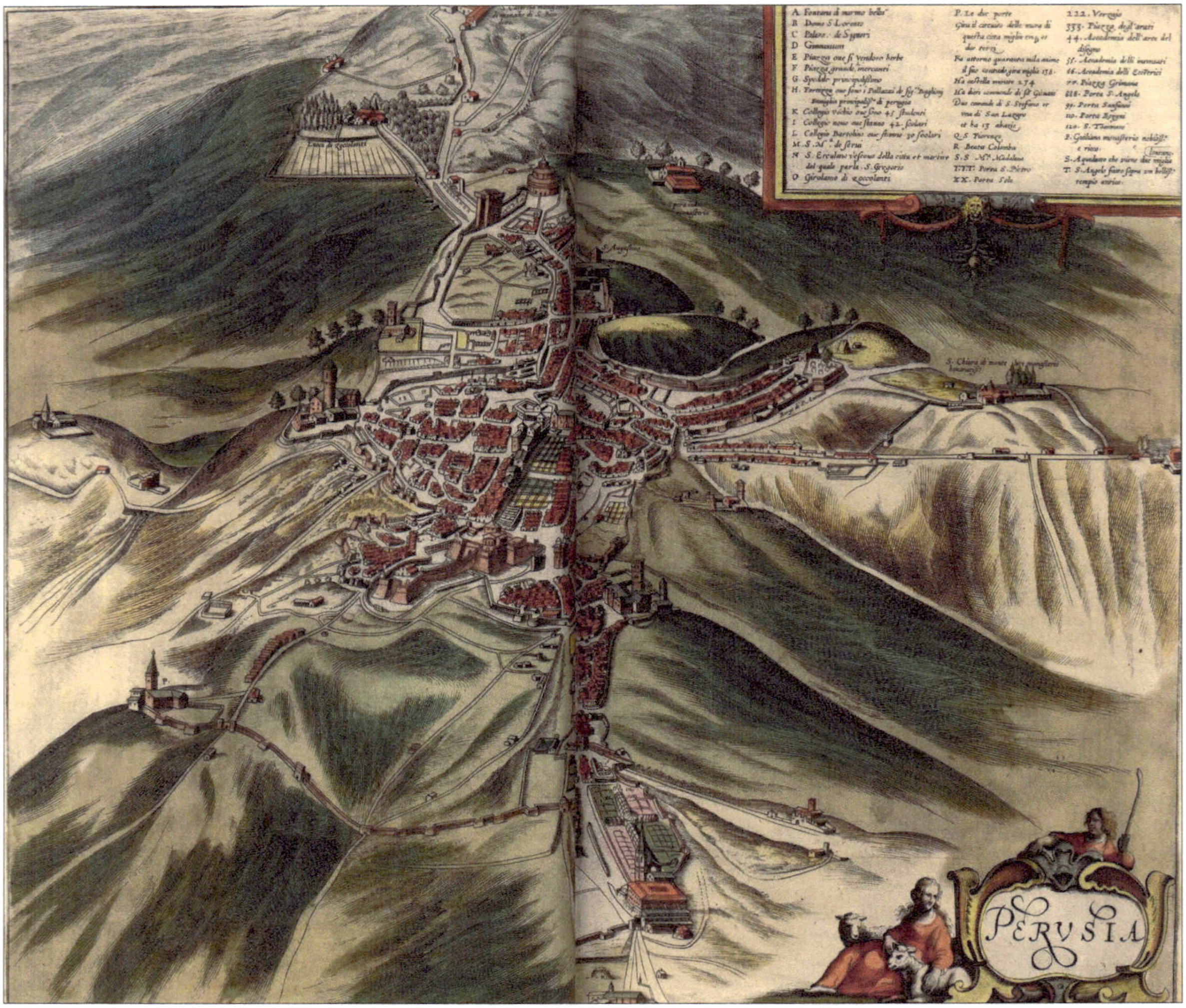

PERUGIA - *Perusia*

ORVIETO

ACQUAPENDENTE

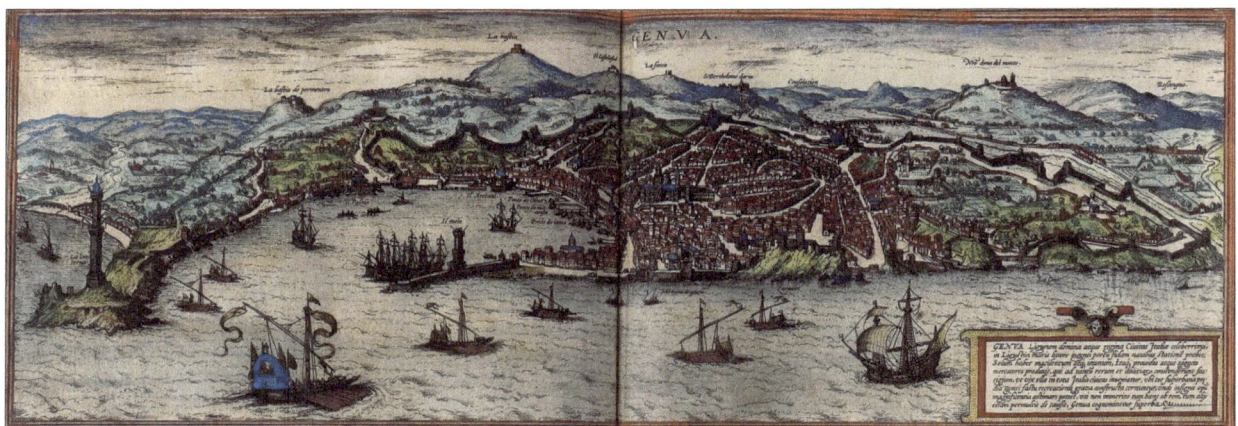

GENOVA

VITERBO - *Viterbium*

CAPRAROLA

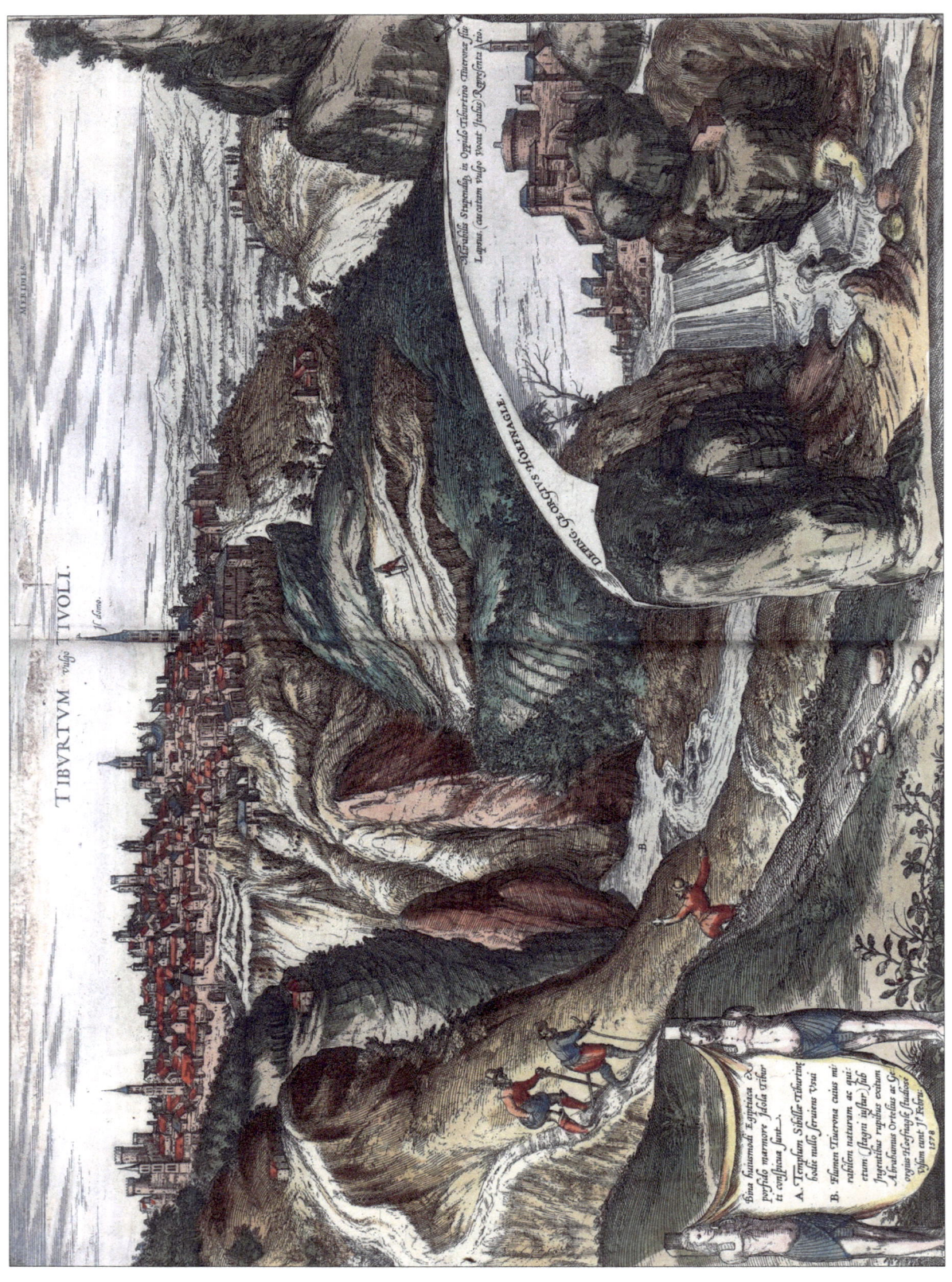

TIVOLI

VELLETRI - *Velitrae*

OSTIA

NETTUNO - *Netuno*

FRASCATI - *Frascate*

FONDI

VETVSTISS. AD MARE THYRRHENVM
TERRACINAE OPPIDVM.

A TERRACINA, olim dicta ANXVR
B Monasterio d. S. Angeli
C Theatrum quadratum
D Antiquorum Arx
E Mare Thyrrhenum
F Via Appia Neapolim Versus
G Divortium, Posterla

DRING GLOR HOEFNA

TERRACINA

GAETA - *Caietae*

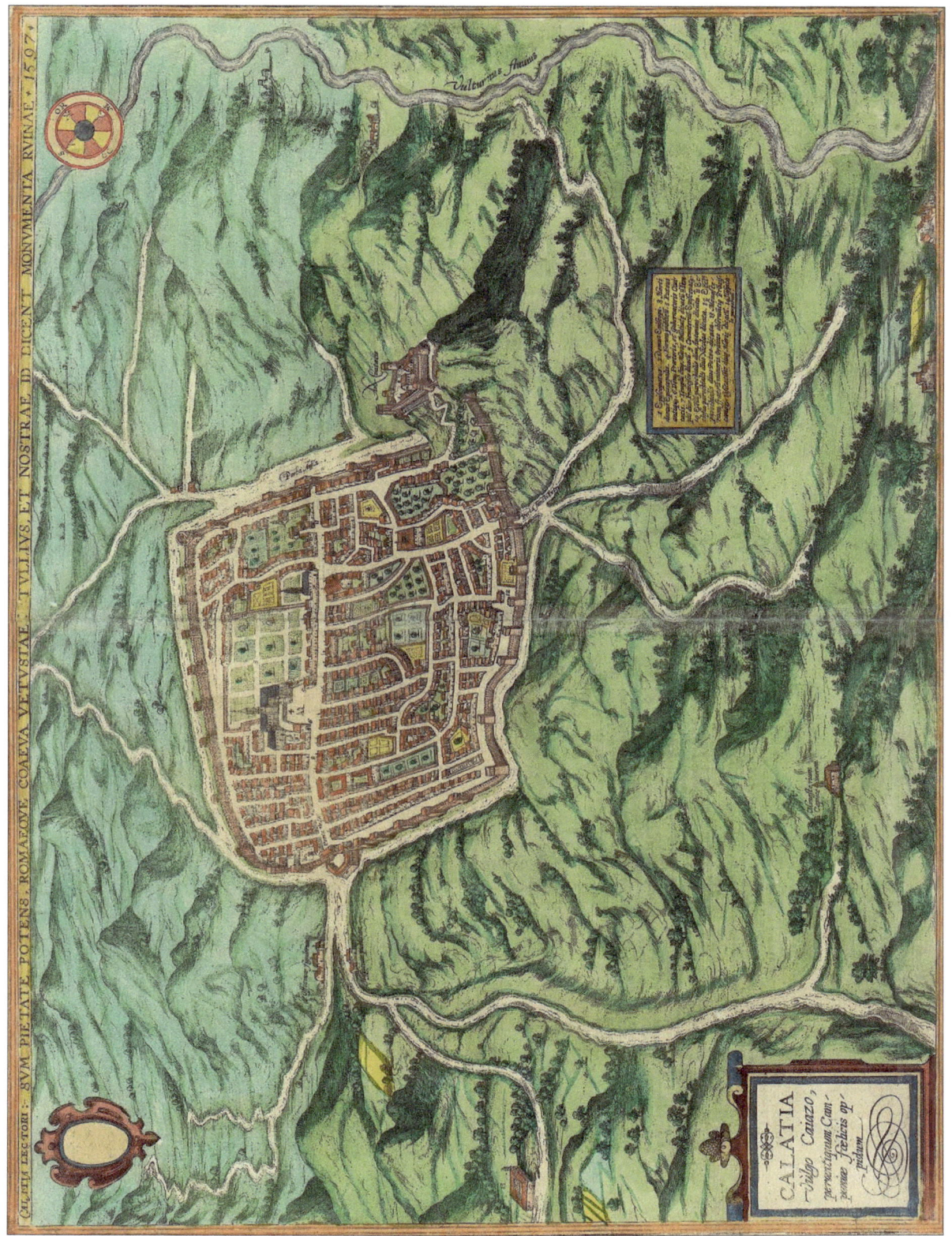

CAIAZZO - Calatia

NAPOLI - *Neapolis*

POZZUOLI - *Puteoli*

TRAPANI

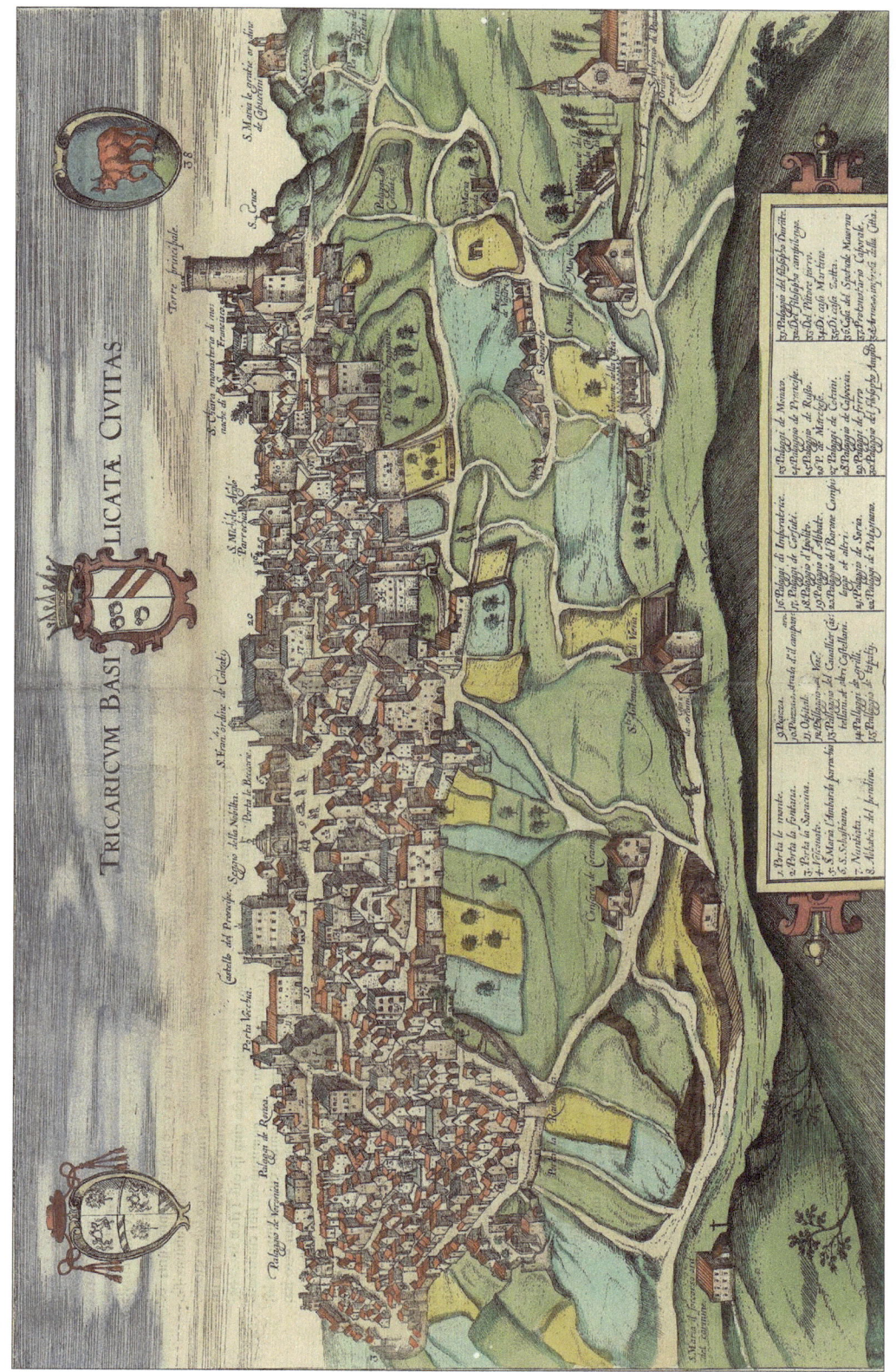

TRICARICO - *Tricaricum*

STRETTO DI MESSINA - *Freti Siculi*

MESSINA - *Messana*

CATANA VRBS SICILIAE CLARISSIMA PATRIA SCTÆ AGATHAE VIRGINIS ET MART:

CATANIA - *Catana*

PALERMO

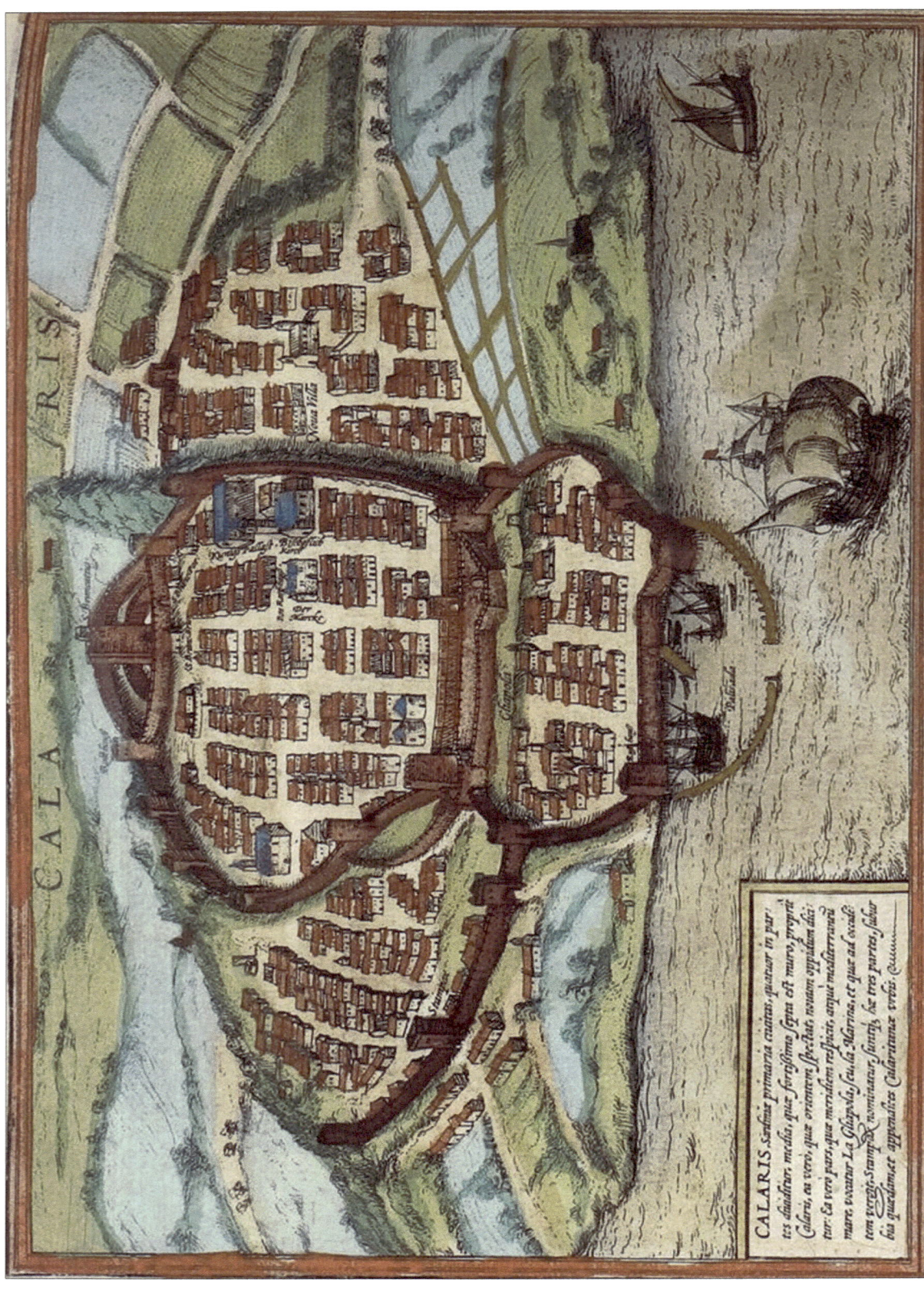

CAGLIARI - *Calaris*

Mediterranean Sea
Mediterraneo

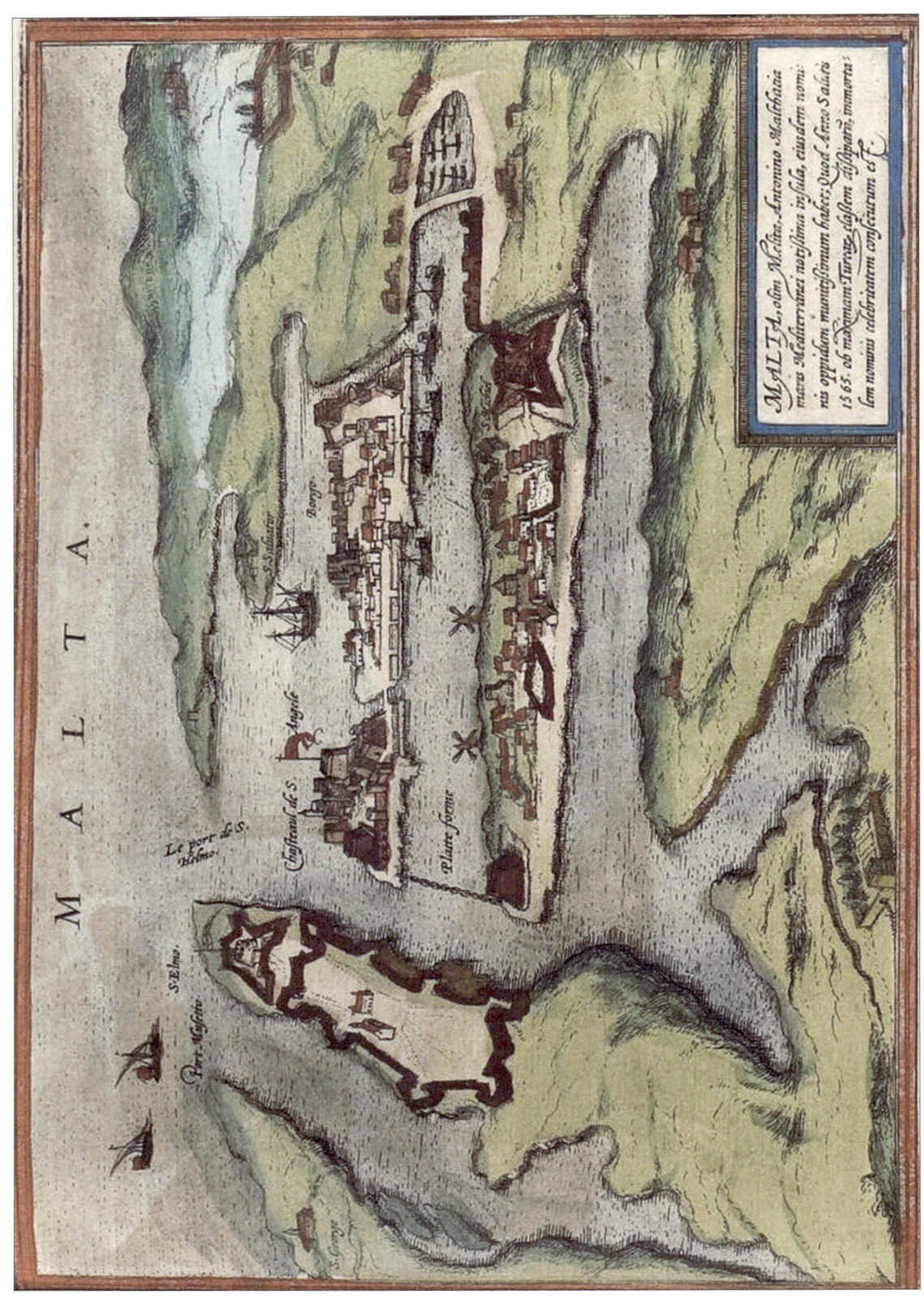

MALTA - LA VALLETTA

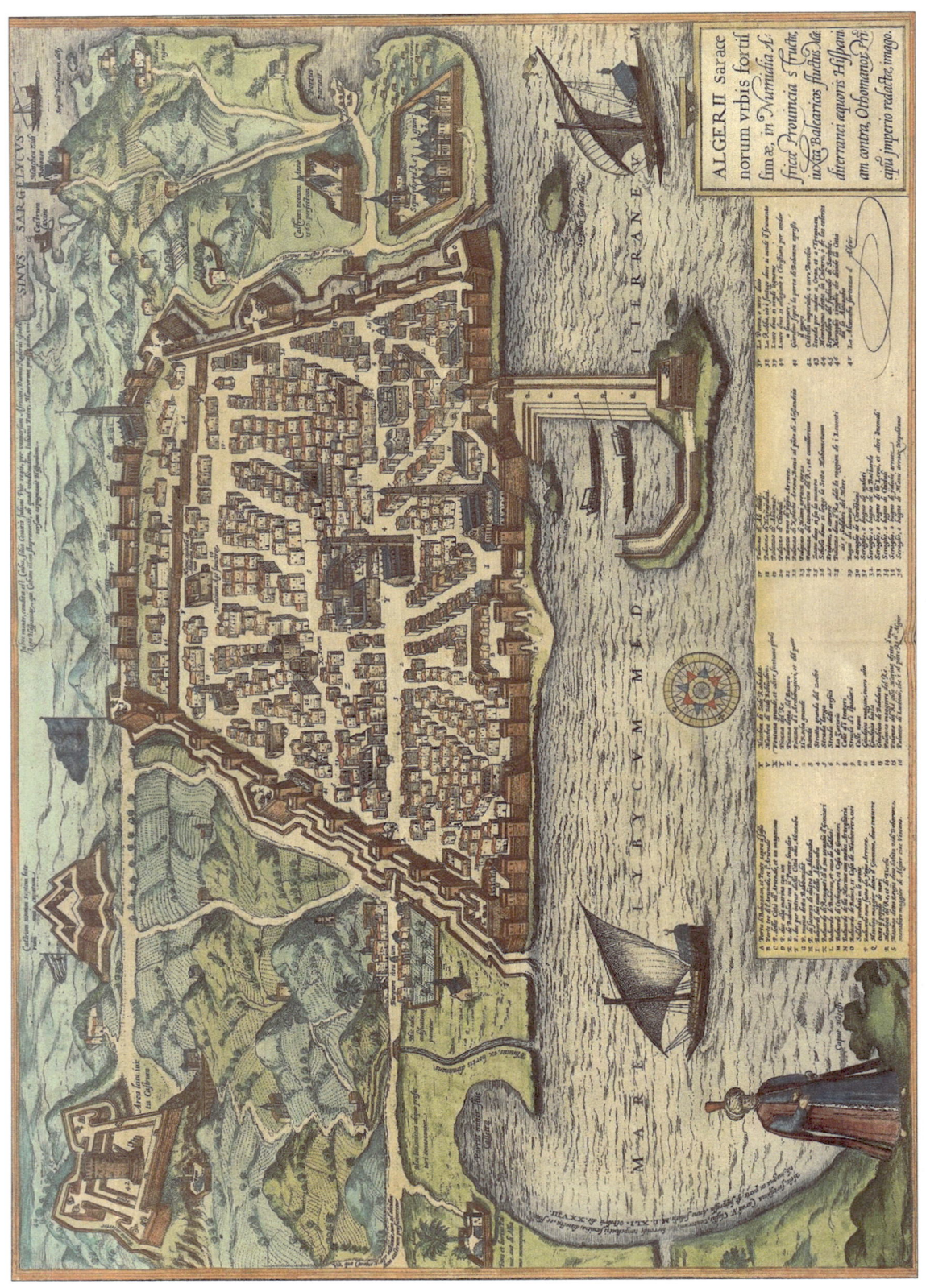

ALGERI - *Algerii*

TUNISI - *Tunes*

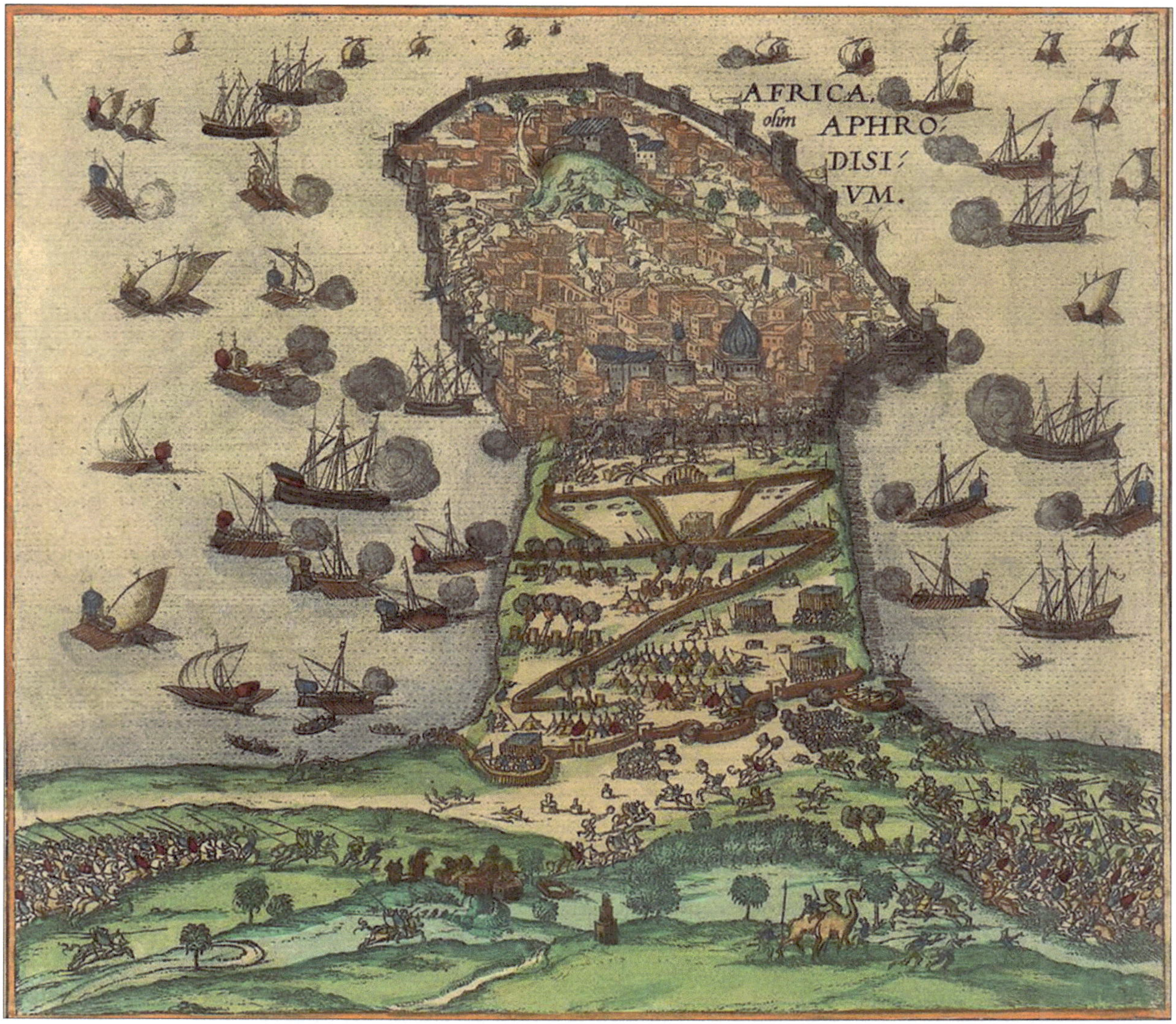

MAHDIA - *Aphrodisium*

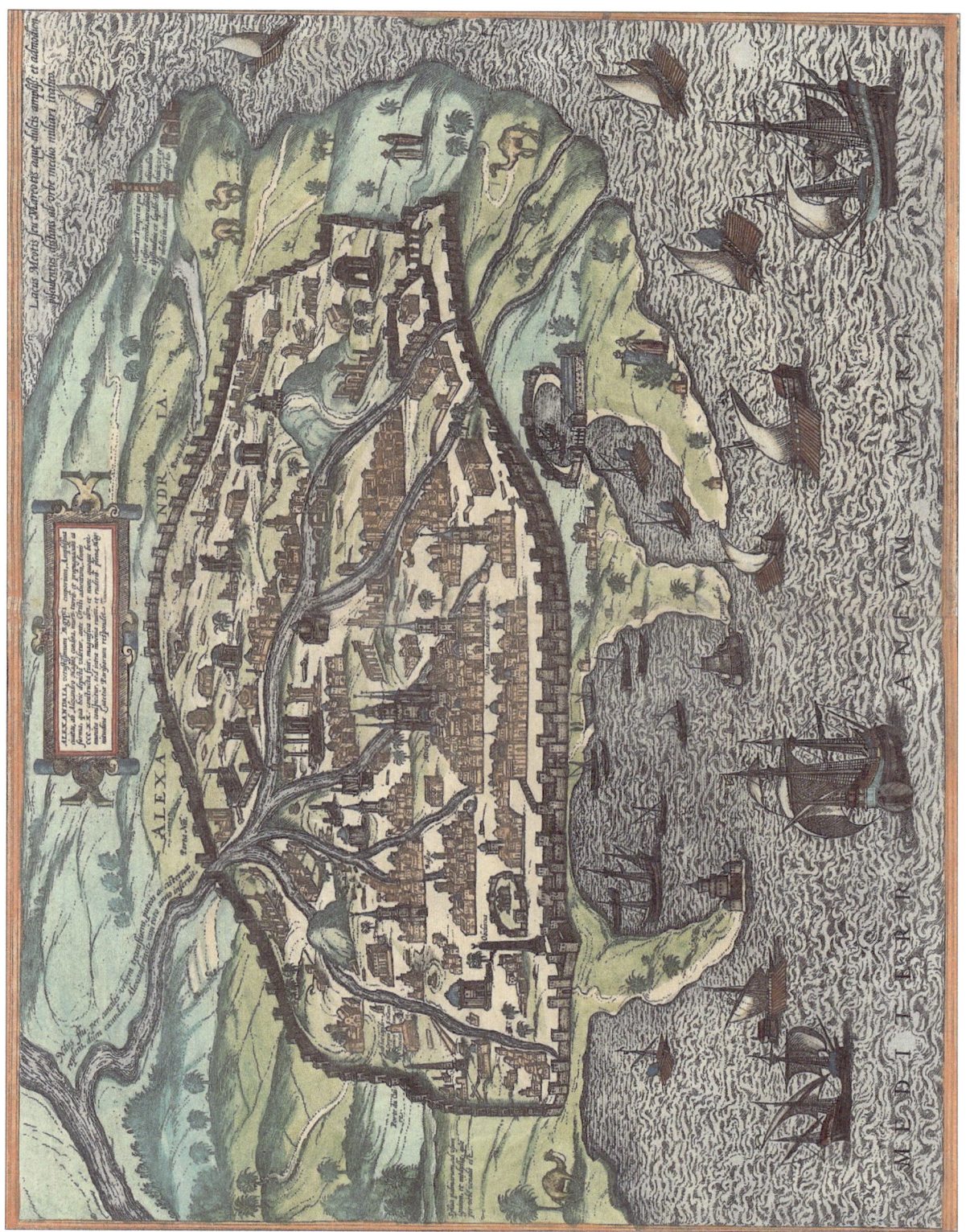

ALESSANDRIA D'EGITTO - *Alexandria*

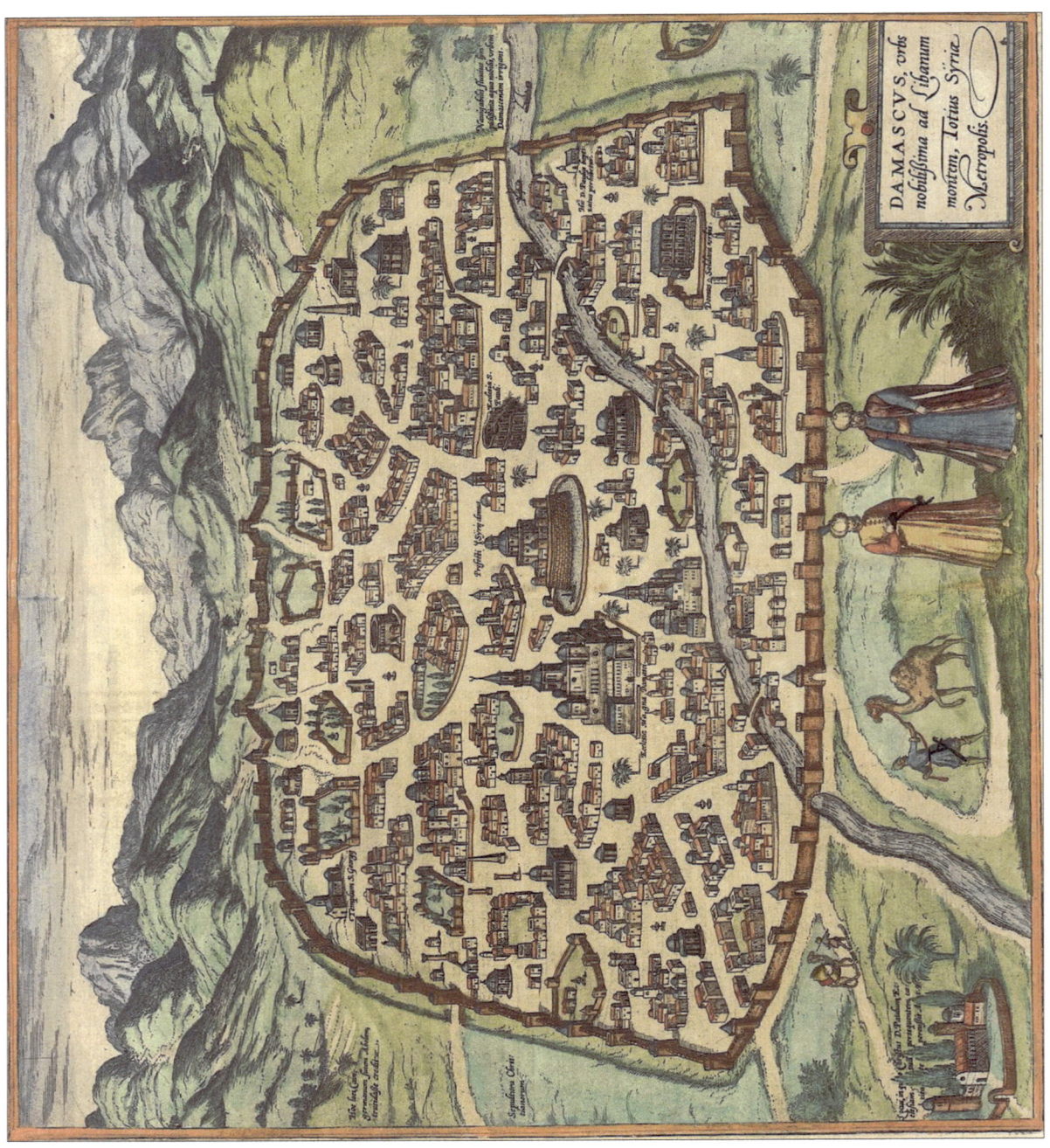

DAMASCO – *Damascus*

GERUSALEMME - *Hyerosolyma*

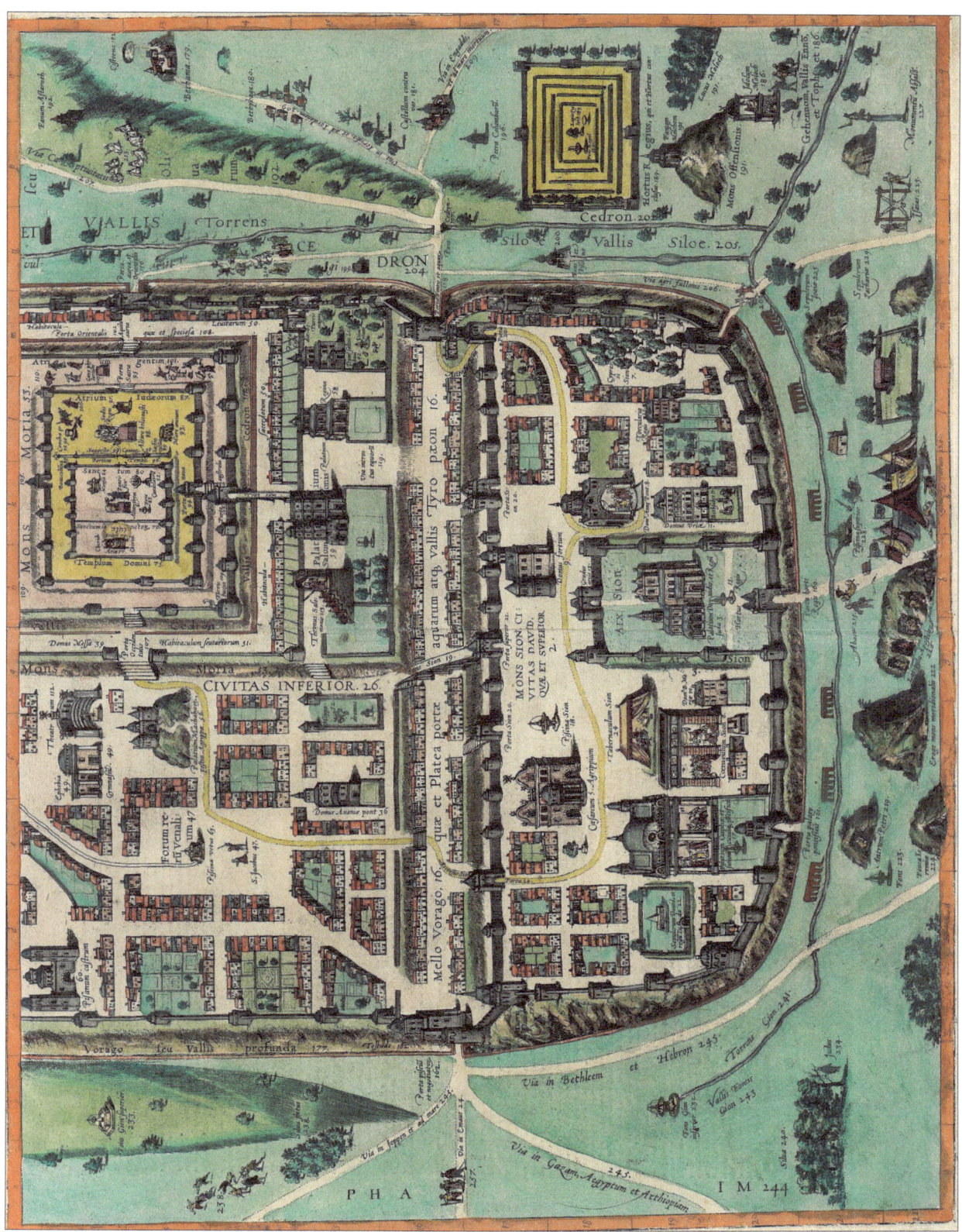

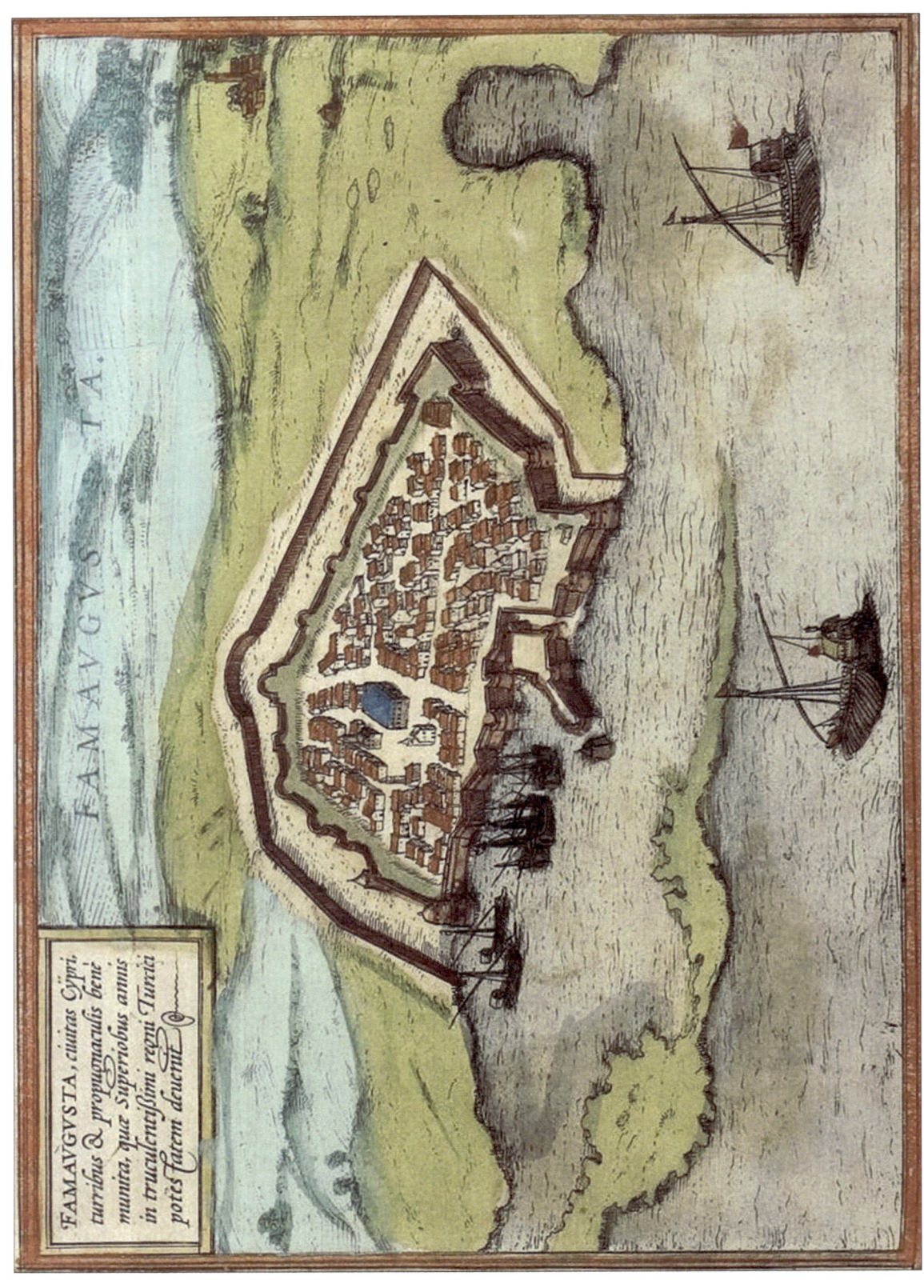

FAMAGOSTA

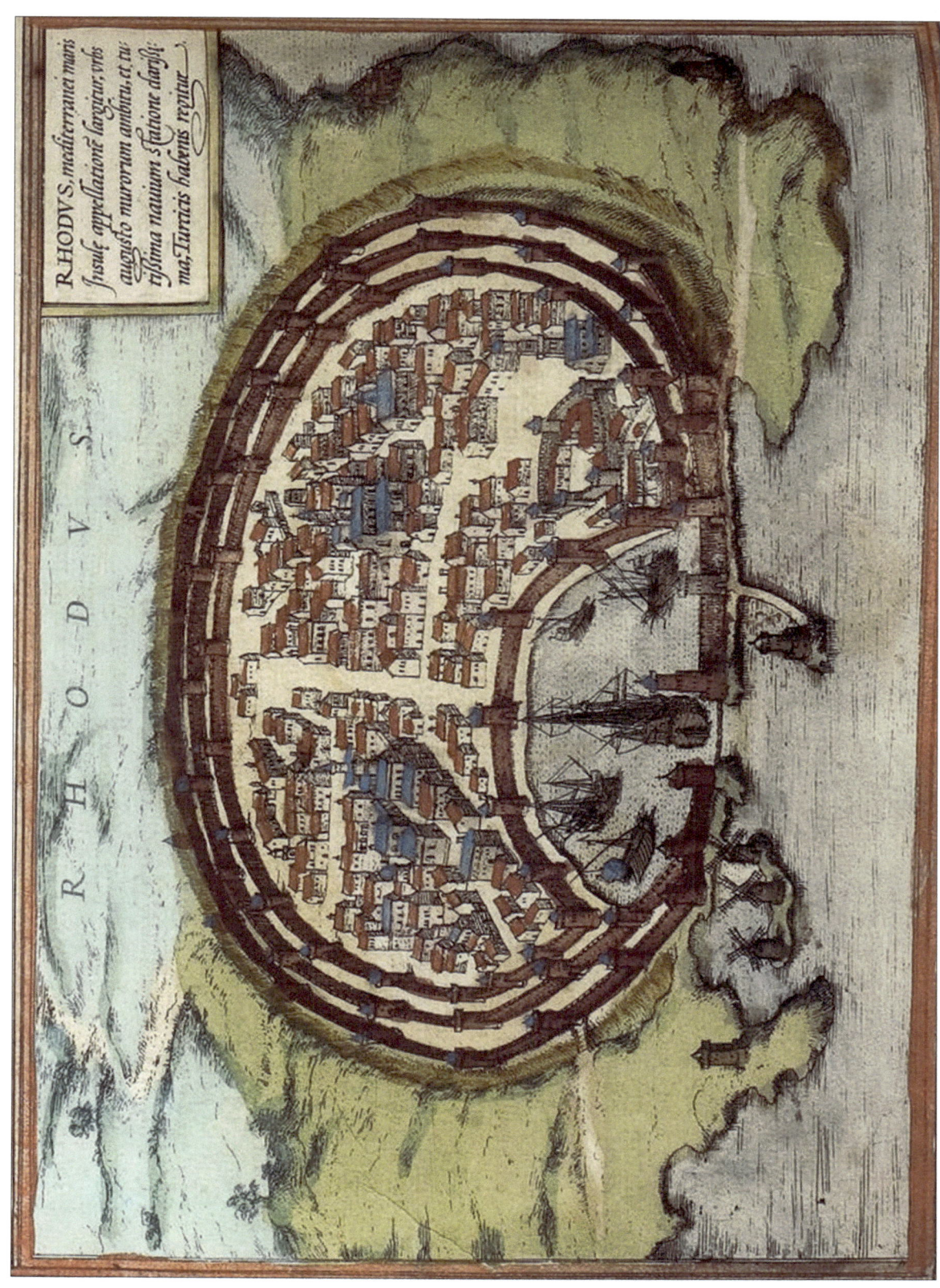

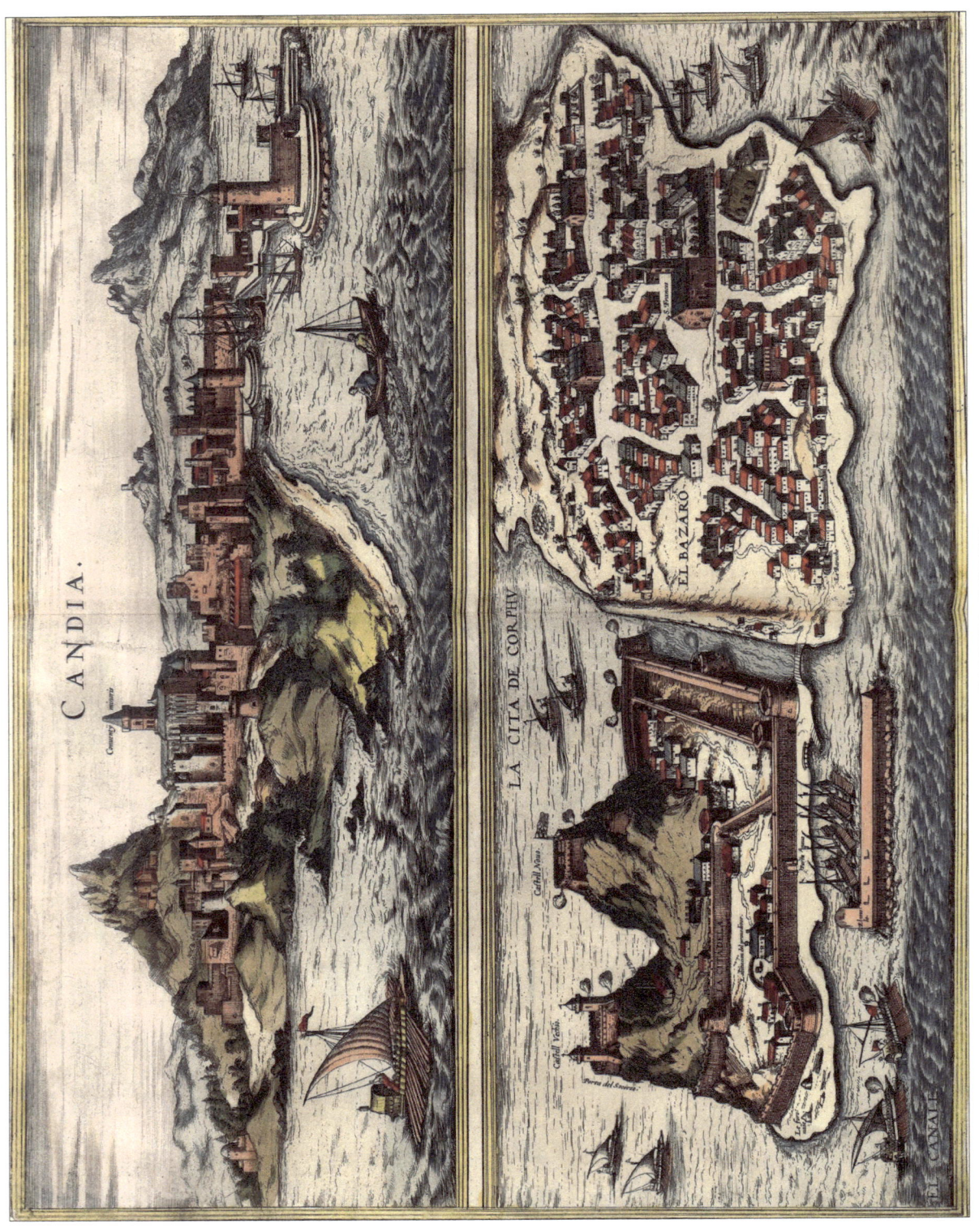

CANDIA CORFU

BABILONIA

BYZANTIUM - COSTANTINOPOLI

SEBENIK PARENZO MODON DALMAZIA

CASTANOWIZ CROAZIA

CONTENTS

INTRODUCTION - THE RISE OF MODERN CARTOGRAPHY   P.5

INTRODUZIONE - NASCITA DELLA CARTOGRAFIA MODERNA   P.9

ITALY - ITALIA P. 13

MEDITERRANEAN SEA'S COSTS P. 77

MUSEUM BOOKS ALREADY PUBLISHED
(SOME TITLES)

 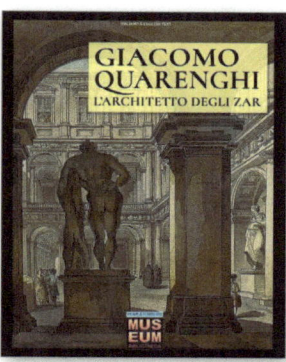 

 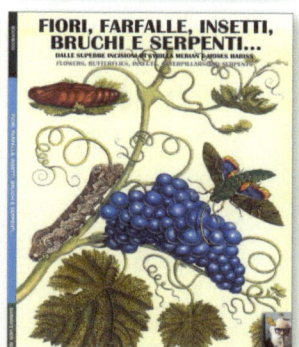 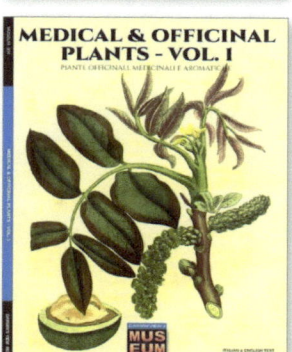

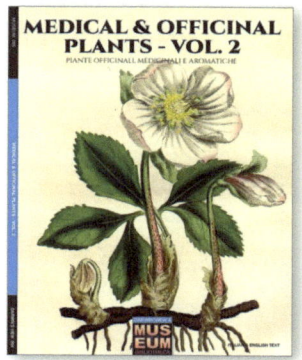  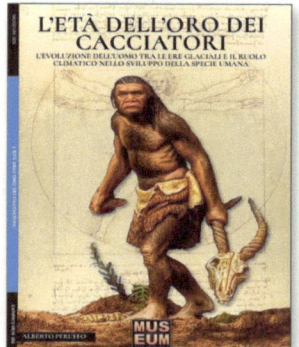

www.ingramcontent.com/pod-product-compliance
Lightning Source LLC
Chambersburg PA
CBHW042308230426
43662CB00033B/55